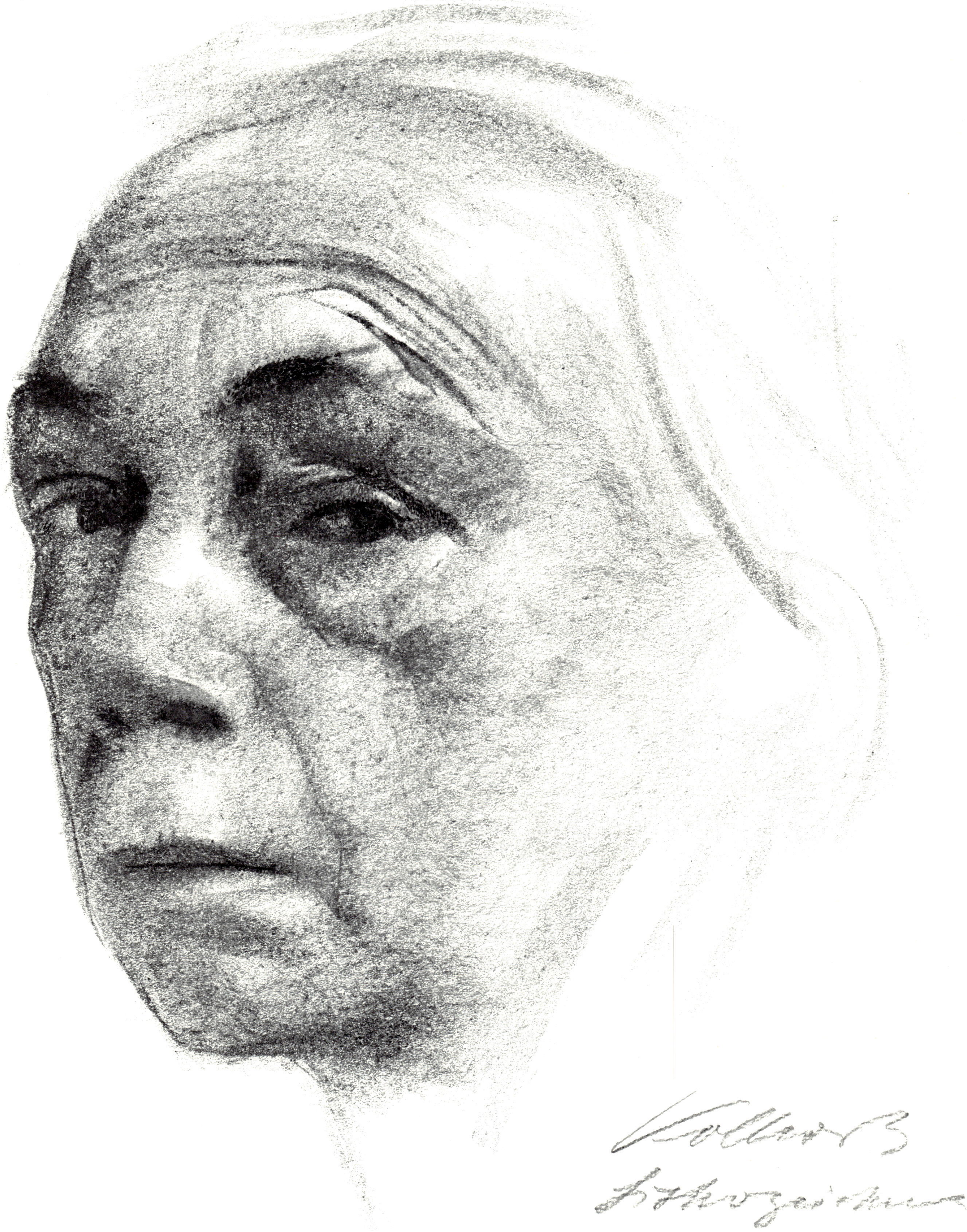

PRINTS AND DRAWINGS OF

Käthe Kollwitz

Selected with Introduction by Carl Zigrosser

DOVER PUBLICATIONS, INC., NEW YORK

Published in Canada by General Publishing Company, Ltd.,
30 Lesmill Road, Don Mills, Toronto, Ontario.
Published in the United Kingdom by Constable and Company, Ltd.,
10 Orange Street, London W.C.2.

This Dover edition, first published in 1969, is a revised
and enlarged version of the work originally published
by George Braziller in 1951 under the title *Kaethe Kollwitz.*

Standard Book Number: 486-22177-6
Library of Congress Catalog Card Number: 73-76286
Manufactured in the United States of America
Dover Publications, Inc.
180 Varick Street
New York, N.Y. 10014

Preface to the Dover Edition

In the preparation of this monograph, I have received much valuable information from people who knew Käthe Kollwitz: Mrs. Fritz Kortner (the artist's niece), Karl Buchholz, George Grosz, Curt Valentin, Dr. August Klipstein, Dr. W. R. Valentiner, and above all Erich Cohn. I am also grateful to Lessing J. Rosenwald and Richard S. Field and the National Gallery of Art in Washington, to Kneeland McNulty and the Philadelphia Museum of Art, to Edgar Breitenbach and Alan Fern of the Library of Congress, to Miss Eleanor Sayre of the Museum of Fine Arts in Boston, to the Galerie St. Etienne in New York, and to Erich Cohn for permission to reproduce pictures; also to Harcourt, Brace and Company for permission to quote from a poem by Carl Sandburg.

This second revised edition contains 83 illustrations, whereas the original edition version had but 72. Most of the illustrations have been rephotographed from the original works of art, and new techniques in photolithography and a larger format have combined to give us reproductions that more closely approximate the prints and drawings themselves. More than a dozen pictures are now shown at full size. My critical estimate of Käthe Kollwitz and her work has not changed since the book was first published in 1946, and so it did not seem necessary or fitting to alter the basic plan and content of my introductory essay. I have, however, made a number of minor alterations in the light of data which were not available when the essay was originally prepared. In addition I have added a bibliography and in the List of Illustrations have given German titles and dimensions of the works reproduced.

Thanks to Dr. Klipstein's admirable catalogue raisonné it is now possible easily to survey the artist's achievement as a whole. One is struck, among other things, by the recurrence and persistence of certain images in the artist's mind. The theme of Death holding a girl in her lap occurs for instance in the woodcut of 1921 (Plate 30) and, with modifications, in the lithograph of 1934 (Plate 69). The image of protecting motherhood appears in the lithograph of 1919 (Plate 28) and the woodcut from the Peasant War sequence of 1923 (Plate 37), and emerges as the Mother Militant protecting the seed corn or future of the human race in her very last lithograph (Plate 64). While the artist was involved with the cycle of Death, the image of the mother bending over the injured child (from the early etching *Run Over* [Plate 25]), came to her mind as a significant gesture of resignation. She made a drawing to represent a *Woman Welcoming Death* (Plate 67). But this conception did not satisfy her, and in the final version she raised the woman's head to look forward and added the frightened children to increase the dramatic effect (Plate 68). Images and themes may have obsessed her, but like a true artist she did not repeat insensitively.

The centenary of the artist's birth occurred on July 8, 1967. I had hoped that this work could have appeared then as a memorial to the occasion. But even though the book appears considerably later, it still can be considered as a centennial tribute. The voice of Käthe Kollwitz still speaks to us with wisdom and compassion in these troubled times.

Philadelphia, Pennsylvania CARL ZIGROSSER
August, 1968

Introduction

The life and work of Käthe Kollwitz were singularly integrated. She was a human being in the fullest sense of the word, and she was a true artist, again in the real meaning of the word, as one who had something to say and said it with memorable power. In her expression she was always true to herself and to her time. Her life was simple and dignified, guided by and dedicated to moral principle. She never compromised her ideals for expediency or monetary success. Her development as an artist was consistent and continuous. She was a searcher to the end. Printmaking was her major interest, sculpture a later and secondary activity. Her drawings, masterly and complete as they are, were always a means to an end, studies for the ultimate print. They were numerous because her own approach to the creative problem demanded preliminary groundwork and clarification. Her choice of printmaking as a vehicle came by inclination and conviction. She understood clearly the aim and purpose of the graphic arts, most democratic of visual media, as the widest distribution of original works at the lowest cost. She did not believe in artificially limiting her editions to give scarcity value. It is by her prints, then, that she is known: a body of some 270 etchings, woodcuts, and lithographs that has brought her international fame.

Käthe Schmidt Kollwitz was born on July 8, 1867, in Königsberg, East Prussia. She grew up in an atmosphere of intense religious feeling, philosophical speculation, and revolutionary thought that left a lasting mark on her character. Her grandfather Julius Rupp, an ordained Lutheran minister, had been expelled from the state church because of certain avowed scruples regarding the Athanasian Creed, and had founded in 1846 the first Free Religious Congregation (Frei-religiöse Gemeinde) in Germany. These groups, in their rejection of the authority of a state religion and in their emphasis on rationalism and ethics, somewhat resemble the Congregationalists and Unitarians in this country. Käthe Kollwitz recalls his personality in a letter to Arthur Bonus: "My grandfather died when I was seventeen years old, and thus I did know him and have a vivid recollection of him. I respected him, but was timid in his presence because I was a bashful child. I did not have the personal relationship with him which my two older sisters and, above all, my brother experienced. Along with the other children of the congregation I had religious instruction under him, an instruction which perhaps passed over the heads of most of the children, myself included. The teaching consisted of religious history, discussion of the gospels, and commentary on the Sunday sermon. A loving God was never brought home to us. *God is Spirit*, *I and the Father are one*, such sayings of Christ made us aware of God. But I did not love God—He was far too remote. I venerated Him, but I loved Jesus. Later when I left the parental home and came under the sway of materialism, I rebelled against all that was called religion. Heinrich Heine's *Here upon a rock we build the Church of the Third New Testament* became for me a real conviction. At least for years. If I for a while believed that the religious force of my grandfather did not live in me, at least there was reverence for his teaching, his personality, and the whole congregation. I might add that in recent years I feel the influence of two generations in me: my father in close proximity, because he served to introduce me to socialism, socialism understood as the much-desired Brotherhood of Man. Behind him stood Rupp, a being linked not to man but to God, the religious man."

From her father Karl Schmidt came, as she says, the impulse toward social responsibility. He had studied law and had practically passed his bar examinations when he came to the conclusion that he could not, with his radical views, hope for advancement in the legal profession as then constituted in Germany. He therefore undertook to learn the mason's trade from the bottom up and became a master-mason. After the death of his father-in-law in 1884, he succeeded him as leader and pastor of the Free Religious Congregation. Käthe Kollwitz made several portaits of her father: an early oil of 1890, a lithograph in 1915 (*The Lonely Man*, K.129), and a lithograph in 1919 of her father and mother (*The Parents of Käthe Kollwitz*, Plate 39). The ravages of time and suffering upon two human beings so graphically depicted in this last picture are pointed up by an early daguerreotype in which they are invested with all the beauty and idealism of youth.

Käthe Schmidt thus grew up in an atmosphere of social and moral idealism. There exists an early photograph of her which already suggests the bent of her character—a quiet, serious child with searching eyes and sad, sensitive mouth. The well-known Kant scholar, Dr. Emil Arnoldt, exerted a certain influence on her spiritual development. She read avidly. Her elder brother, Konrad, introduced her to Goethe and the revolutionary poems of Freiligrath. The chief urge, however, was to art. She later told Max Lehrs that she had been destined by her father even as a child (for she had shown marked aptitude) for an art career even though "unfortunately" she came into the world as a girl. She recalled the impression made upon her by a volume of Hogarth's engravings—which has a certain significance in view of her later devotion to printmaking. At the age of thirteen she received her first formal instruction in drawing from Rudolph Mauer, an erstwhile pupil of Mandel, the old reproductive engraver, and it was Mauer later who first initiated her in the technique of etching and intaglio printing. A year's trial at art school in Berlin was decided upon. In 1885, at the age of eighteen, she went to Berlin in company with her brother, who was studying literature and political economy at the University. It is related by Kämmerer that one of the first places to which her brother took her was the burial place (Märzfriedhof, Friedenhain) of those killed in the "March Revolution." The Revolution of 1848 was a great tradition not only in her family from grandfather Rupp on (who had preached a memorial in 1848) but also among the workers of Berlin. She made two lithographs of the subject in 1913 (K.123, 124) and mentioned how she often visited the scene.

She studied with Karl Stauffer-Bern, and through him she first discovered the prints of Max Klinger, whose naturalistic dramatizations of contemporary life in print sequence form, *A Glove*, *Dramas*, *A Life*, were much discussed. On the whole, however, the art life of the German capital was far less lively and stimulating than that of Munich, to which she went in 1888 after an interval of two years at home. In addition to her studies at the Herterich Academy, there were exciting discoveries in literature and drama: the impact of Zola, Ibsen, and Björnson. Her brother recalled that Arne Garborg's *From a Man's World* made a specially deep impression on her. She herself has spoken of a lecture by August Bebel which prompted her to read his book, *Women, Past, Present, and Future*, and which was the beginning of her conscious interest in social democracy and the related feminist movement.

In 1891 she married Dr. Karl Kollwitz, a boyhood friend of her brother, and settled down at 25 Weissenburger St., Berlin, N.58, the house in which she was to live practically all her life. Dr. Kollwitz was a *Kassenarzt*, a title for which there is no English equivalent. He maintained a kind of clinic or dispensary, open to subscribers of a small weekly sum. It was a form of medical insurance, developed in Germany far in advance of other countries. Needless to say, a doctor who practiced socialized medicine in a workingman's district had no ambition to amass a fortune; Dr. Kollwitz shared his wife's dedication to social service. In 1892 her first son Hans was born. She had by no means, however, given up her art. For several years she had been drawing and painting independently, and was becoming more and more attracted to etching. Line, and not color, was to be the keynote of her expression. The graphic arts seemed most appropriate to delineate the social flux in which Germany found itself. She had already learned the rudiments of the craft. She now set about, from 1890 onward, to acquire a mastery of etching technique. The first prints were largely fragmentary, a study of a hand or face, based upon herself as a model, following Rembrandt's practice. She was learning the use of ground and needle and acid, the wiping of ink, the mysteries of aquatint as in the *Self Portrait at Table*, 1893 (Plate 2). She was perfecting herself in observation, the rendering of flesh and form, the interplay of light and shadow, studies in unflinching realism, *Female Nude* (K.3), *Male Nude* (K.4), studies in expressing feelings or grouping figures, as in the charming little etching *Greeting* of 1892 (Plate 1) or in *Tavern Interior* (K.12). She exhibited publicly for the first time in 1893.

Having attained some degree of control over the means of expression, she began to explore subject matter in what might be called studies in social drama. Käthe Kollwitz was, I believe, fundamentally a dramatic artist who dealt in human emotions and who evoked them with great subtlety through gesture and facial expression. She had the power of suggesting overtones, of rendering feelings corporeal. Her conception often overflowed the bounds of a single print into a cycle of related prints unfolding a dramatic sequence. In this connection her early liking for Hogarth is illuminating because he too made such use of interrelated series in *Rake's Progress* or *Marriage à la Mode*. In her earlier phase she sometimes used a book or a play as the springboard for her creative idea. The pictures thus indirectly inspired were not really illustrations of literary themes. It was rather that she used the dramatic idea or situation as raw material which she transmuted into pictures in her own plastic terms, just as Rembrandt used the Bible story as the stimulus or source of his own imaginative reconstructions. The first of these dramatic renderings was a scene from *Germinal* of 1894 (K.21) inspired by Zola's novel, and depicting the fight between Lantier and Chaval at the inn.

A far more powerful stimulus to the imagination was the production of Gerhart Hauptmann's play, *The Weavers*, first performed at the Berliner Freie Bühne in the winter of 1893. The play dramatized the desperate plight and revolt in 1840 of the Silesian weavers, who earned a precarious living with hand looms. These disturbances in the 1840s were really part of the great industrial revolution which swept Europe, a conflict between the factory and the home, the power loom and handwork. Inspired by the play, and possibly by additional study of historical sources—for her conception differs somewhat from Hauptmann's drama—she undertook to create her own dramatic sequence. She worked on it from 1894 to 1898, a period of intense creative activity. Study after study was made, etching after etching was completed only to be rejected and done over again, until her conception, now refined and clarified, found concrete embodiment in the set of six prints, the Weavers (Plates 3–8). The episodes follow a dramatic pattern of provocation, angry reaction, and tragic end: poverty, death, conspiracy, procession of angry weavers, storming the owner's house, death by soldiers' rifle in the weaver's home. It was a landmark of class-conscious art: for almost the first time the plight of the worker and his age-long struggle to better his position received sympathetic treatment in pictures. The set was first shown in the big Berlin Art Exhibition of 1898 and caused quite a sensation. The artists' jury of award, including the aged Menzel and Liebermann, proposed it for the gold medal, but this honor was vetoed by the Emperor. The Berlin Print Cabinet purchased a set, but the sale was not publicized in deference to the Emperor, who was violently opposed to all art of social content—"gutter art" (*Rinnsteinkunst*) was what he called it. Nevertheless, the Weavers set, exhibited in 1899 at Dresden, was awarded a gold medal there, and also received a prize at London in 1900.

Käthe Kollwitz was now established as an artist to be seriously considered. While she was working on the Weavers she had also produced in addition to many drawings several self portraits, a symbolic plate with two completed studies thereto (rejected, and rightly so, for the final subject of the Weavers cycle), a *Portrait of Her Son Hans* (K.30), the first lithograph, and the powerfully realized etching of the *Woman with Folded Hands* (Plate 11). This creative activity is rather amazing when one considers that her first son Hans was born in September 1892 and her second son Peter in February 1896. She successfully resolved the dilemma which confronts every woman artist. She produced both children and works of art; and both were good. A family servant made it possible for her to work every morning in her studio. As her niece, Mrs. Kortner, wrote: "Please stop this legend that she had no servants. It would hopelessly discourage those women who struggle in vain to manage husband, children, household, and do something besides. By the way the household was not at all bohemian; it was clean and very tidy, almost puritan-like."

From 1902 to 1908 she worked on her second great print cycle, the Peasant War (Plates 15–21). But before and during those years she also produced a number of other works: *Gretchen*, the pregnant girl who sees shame and death reflected in the water below (K.42, 43), *The Downtrodden* (Plate 13), her second and last excursion into the obvious symbolism of Klinger, and *La Carmagnole* (Plate 10), the dance around the guillotine, a historical reconstruction inspired, it is said, by Dickens' *A Tale of Two Cities*. This last etching marked perhaps the height of her realistic phase; in fact it was too realistically elaborate. The detail which she lavished on the buildings in the background and on the cobblestones in the foreground tended to detract from the central drama of character, which in turn seemed almost too strained and melodramatic. In contrast to this was the monumental *Mother with Dead Child* (Plate 14), a shattering study of a mother's grief on its most primitive and savage level. During this period, too, she made various experiments in lithographic effects with tusche, crayon, scraping, and transfer, including the sensitive *Working Woman's Profile Left* (K.67) and several lithographs printed in color, most striking of which is the *Woman with Blue Shawl* (Plate 12).

The dramatic curve of the Peasant War cycle corresponds almost exactly with that of the Weavers. In each there was a statement of the provoking causes, a reaction to them, an outbreak of violence, followed by defeat and death. The two great classes of the downtrodden in the past, the peasant and the worker, were thus shown to have had a common pattern in their groping toward a better life. She probably obtained her historical documentation for the Peasant War from Zimmermann's and Bebel's studies on the subject. In Germany during the early sixteenth century, there was considerable oppressive exploitation of the peasantry, and the ensuing revolts, marred by excesses on both sides, were eventually crushed with savage brutality. From this turbulent picture Käthe Kollwitz built up a sequence which portrayed the peasant's lot. The seven plates, all of them intaglio and with complicated techniques, were larger than the Weavers set, the canvas broader. Yet not all were equally successful. The first, *Plowing* (Plate 15), is almost too melodramatic, yet possibly in no other way could the poverty of the serf be so graphically presented. The second *Raped* (Plate 16), is unconvincing, almost Klingeresque, and suffers from a fatal elaboration of background. The third, *Sharpening the Scythe* (Plate 17), in which the peasant woman broods over her wrongs, is a masterpiece of psychological suggestion. The fourth, *Seizing Arms* (Plate 18), is a masterly exposition of violent action, as is the next print, *Outbreak* (Plate 19), in which the angry peasant woman is shown inciting the mob. The sixth, *After the Battle* (Plate 20), in minor key, shows the stoical search of the mother for her dead son. The final episode, *The Prisoners* (Plate 21), wherein they await their doom with varying degrees of resignation, is the tragic anticlimax of the Peasant War.

It is interesting to note that the protagonist of four of the seven acts of this drama is a woman. This urge to voice the basic attitude of woman was to find even more complete expression in Käthe Kollwitz as time went on. Yet it was not so much as woman but as mother that she looked at life. Her allegiance was not to Aphrodite but to the Eternal Mother. In none of her works is a trace of alluring or sophisticated sex. She expressed feminine sensibility with masculine direct-

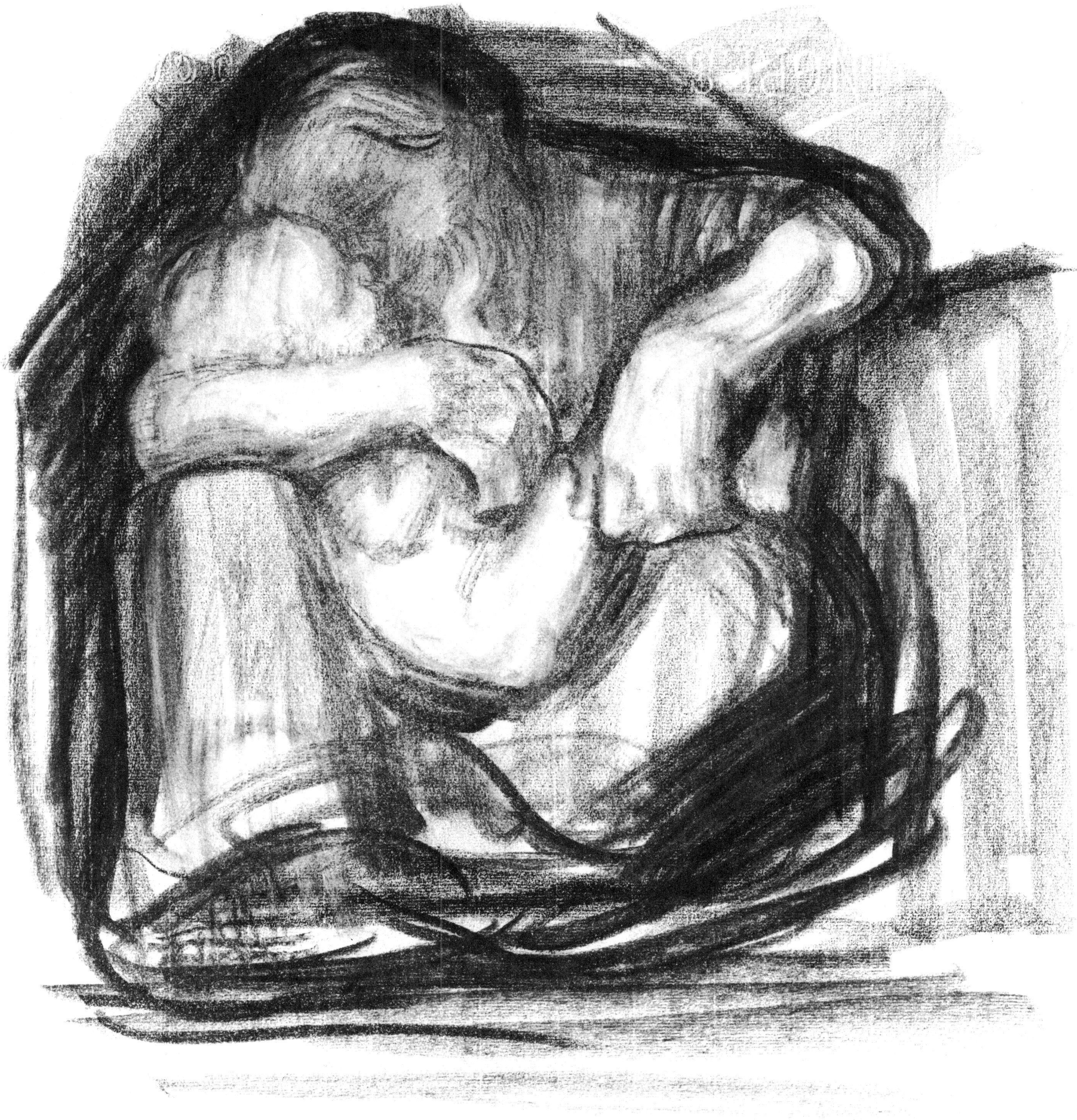

1. Woman with Child in Lap

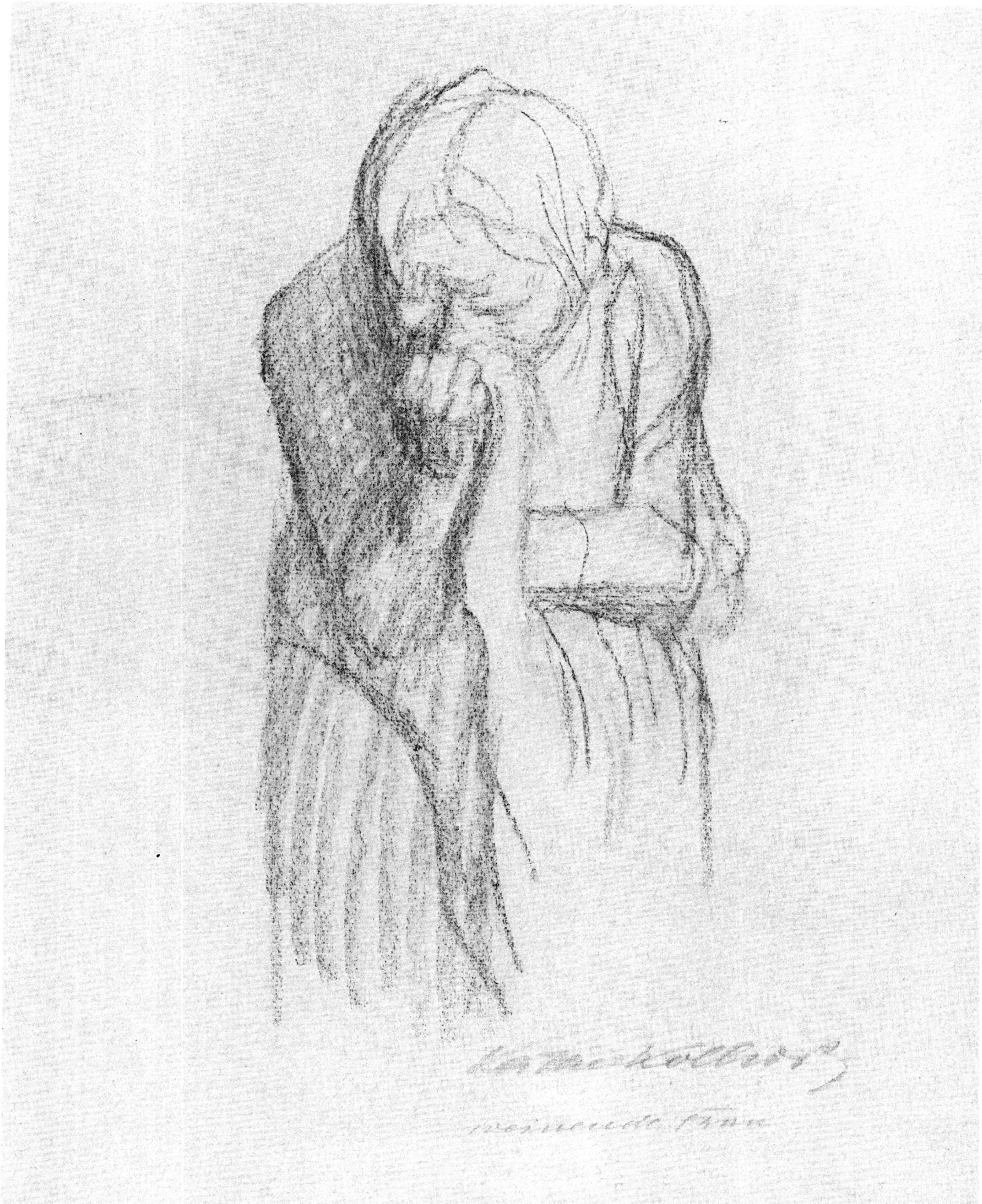

11. Weeping Woman

ness, or perhaps one should say, with the plainspokenness of elemental woman—the matriarch—on whom tactics of subtle indirection had not yet been imposed by society. This maternal viewpoint is one of her great contributions, and she takes her place among the growing body of modern artists (for it is a modern phenomenon) whose utterance is valid, not as an imitation of what man has already done very well, but as an authentic voice of womankind.

The set of the Peasant War was published in 1908 under the auspices of the Society for Historical Art; and, furthermore, gained for her the award of the Villa Romana Prize, endowed by Max Klinger, which carried with it the privilege of a year's residence at the Villa Romana in Florence. Italy with its classical heritage, however, had little influence upon her thought and art. Like Barlach and Grosz she was essentially a Gothic artist, in whom idealized beauty and balance were subordinated to emotional expressiveness. As Gerhart Hauptmann once wrote: "Her silent lines penetrate the marrow like a cry of pain; such a cry was never heard among the Greeks and Romans." One would not suspect that the etching, *Woman and Death* (Plate 23), was made in 1910 after her return from Italy. It is one of her most moving and powerful designs, superb in draftsmanship and technical execution. The year 1910 was a fruitful one, for it included such important prints as the *Self Portrait with Hand on Brow* (K.106), the soft-ground etching *Run Over* (Plate 25), two of her best studies of types: *Woman with Earring* (K.105) and *Pregnant Woman* (K.108), and the charming little etching *Mother with Child in Arms* (Plate 26).

Arthur Bonus suggests that after the outburst of 1910 her creative powers went into partial eclipse until about 1919, though he offers no reason. J. Müller says that illness and the impact of the war affected her adversely from 1914 to 1918. Whatever the reason, the period was relatively unproductive. The five essays in etching she made during 1911, for example, all preoccupied with the theme of the mother with the dead child, were singularly uninspired and unsuccessful. It may well be, too that she had carried the etching technique as far as it could go; it no longer was a challenge to her. She needed a new approach, a new orientation. Her *Self Portrait* of 1912 (K.122) is notable as a step in the simplification of form. The snow white hair of the later portraits appears for the first time. Her later work with but few exceptions was in lithography or woodcut. About 1910 she began also to work in sculpture. World War I was a great blow to her, and involved her in a personal loss. Her younger son, then eighteen, volunteered and was killed at Dixmuiden, Flanders, in October 1914. The following year she began to work on a sculptured memorial to fallen volunteers. This she could never bring to completion and it was destroyed along with other early plastic works. In 1924 she began a new version which was eventually placed (1932) in the soldiers' cemetery of Eessen-Roggeveld near Dixmuiden. The two life-size figures of the sorrowing *Mother* and *Father*, actually portraits of herself and her husband, are perhaps her most important sculptures. Echoes of the war years may also be felt in the lithograph of 1914, *Waiting* (K.126), and in several others executed a little later, including *The Mothers* (Plate 28), likewise a study in anxious waiting, and *Killed in Action* (Plate 46).

Her fiftieth birthday was honored by a large retrospective show at the Paul Cassirer Gallery in 1917. The establishment of the Weimar Republic lifted the restrictions which had been imposed by imperial prejudice. In 1919 she was elected to the Berlin Academy of Art (the most important organization in Germany because it was state-supported) and given the title of Professor. Such a title carried with it more prestige in Germany than it might elsewhere, and also the privilege of a free studio in the Academy building. She was the first woman to be elected to the Academy.

About 1919, then, one senses the rekindling of the creative urge in her. Her style had changed. The aim of realism to capture the particular and accidental with minute exactness was abandoned for a more abstract and universal conception and a more summary execution. It is a logical development in an artist's career, exactly paralleled in the earlier and later phases of a draftsman like Daumier, for example. After an artist has been through the discipline and has mastered the details of visual form, then only does he know what is essential and what can be left out. Then he is free to stylize for monumental effect or inner truth. No doubt physical factors also play a part in the artist's change of attitude. When his eyes are no longer capable of encompassing minute detail, he seeks to conquer new problems with the visual knowledge and spiritual maturity of a lifetime.

There were many reflections of the feverish and tragic postwar years of Germany in Käthe Kollwitz's work. It was not the Germany of Grosz, Beckmann, Kirchner, and the rest. It was her own milieu of humble folk beset by hunger, sickness, and despair. Thus inflation and unemployment carried out their grim liquidation. There was the old man who had no recourse left but the noose (*The Last Resort*, Plate 57), the variations on the theme of hunger: the bloated figure of *Starvation* (K.169), the mother choking off her children's cry (*Bread!*, Plate 49), the mutely desperate beseeching *Beggars* (K.193), the whole story again epitomized in the Proletariat trilogy, *Unemployment* (K.206), *Hunger* (K.207), and *Infant Mortality* (Plate 56). These are among her most distressing and painful works. The spectator's credulity and emotions seem strained to the uttermost. Yet the scenes were not unduly exaggerated; the times were indeed desperate. There was also a reminiscence of political turbulence, one of the few examples in her oeuvre, the *Karl Liebknecht Memorial* of 1919 (Plate 29). Liebknecht was a friend of the family. His father Wilhelm Liebknecht had been editor of *Vorwärts*, the socialist paper, until his death in 1900. Käthe's brother Konrad often contributed to it and other socialist magazines. Karl Liebknecht was a socialist deputy in the Reichstag, and one of the few who stood out against the war in 1914 even to the extent of going to prison. Later with Rosa Luxemburg he became leader of the Spartacus party, rose against the majority socialists under Scheidemann, was again imprisoned in 1919 and shot "while escaping." The woodcut, one of the first she made, showed the grief-stricken workers filing past his bier.

Part of her reflections on the grim sequel of war in Germany took the form in 1923 of a set of seven woodcuts entitled War (Plates 32–38). It was her most important work in that medium. She made in all only about thirty woodcuts, chiefly during the years 1922 to 1926. It has been said that her woodcuts were influenced by Barlach. It is difficult to see any similarity. Barlach's woodcuts and lithographs were strongly stylized, the apt expression of his own very personal way of seeing. They were essentially linear, a translation on wood of a pen line. Her own approach was quite different, stressing mass and heavy accents rather than line, the dark areas being relieved by delineation in white line and giving suggestion of color through variations of semitones. It was a rather common idiom of the day, employed by such artists as Kirchner, Nolde, Schmidt-Rottluff, Pechstein, and Heckel, and stemming probably from the example of Gauguin and Munch. As usual, a tremendous amount of preliminary work was expended before she hit upon the final form. In *Das neue Kollwitz Werk* she wrote, "I started the war series as etchings but was not satisfied with the results. I therefore destroyed all but these two [*The Widow*, K.131, and *The Mothers*, K.134]. Whereupon I tried a few lithographs on the same theme [*The Mothers*, Plate 28, *The Parents*, K.144, and *The Widow*, K.160]. In the end I found the most satisfactory interpretation in woodcut."

The cycle War represented the reaction of woman as wife and mother to war. During the growth of the conception, through all its transmutations in drawings, etchings, and lithographs, it was abstracted of all extraneous detail, and finally emerged as a pure drama of emotional tensions. It was closely knit, plastic, and monumental in form, universal in feeling. The first two blocks, *The Sacrifice* and *The Volunteers* (Plates 32 and 33), were in an ecstatic mood of dedication and idealistic self-sacrifice. The next three, *The Parents*, *The Widow, I; The Widow, II* (Plates 34–36), registered despair in descending key. The sixth, *The Mothers* (Plate 37), was a summing up of the aftermath of war. The final block, *The People* (Plate 38), was an affirmation of faith, symbolized by the mother shielding her offspring, and plagued by phantoms of hate, poverty, and ignorance. She stands there steadfast: woman as creator, *Mater-Genetrix*, begetter of

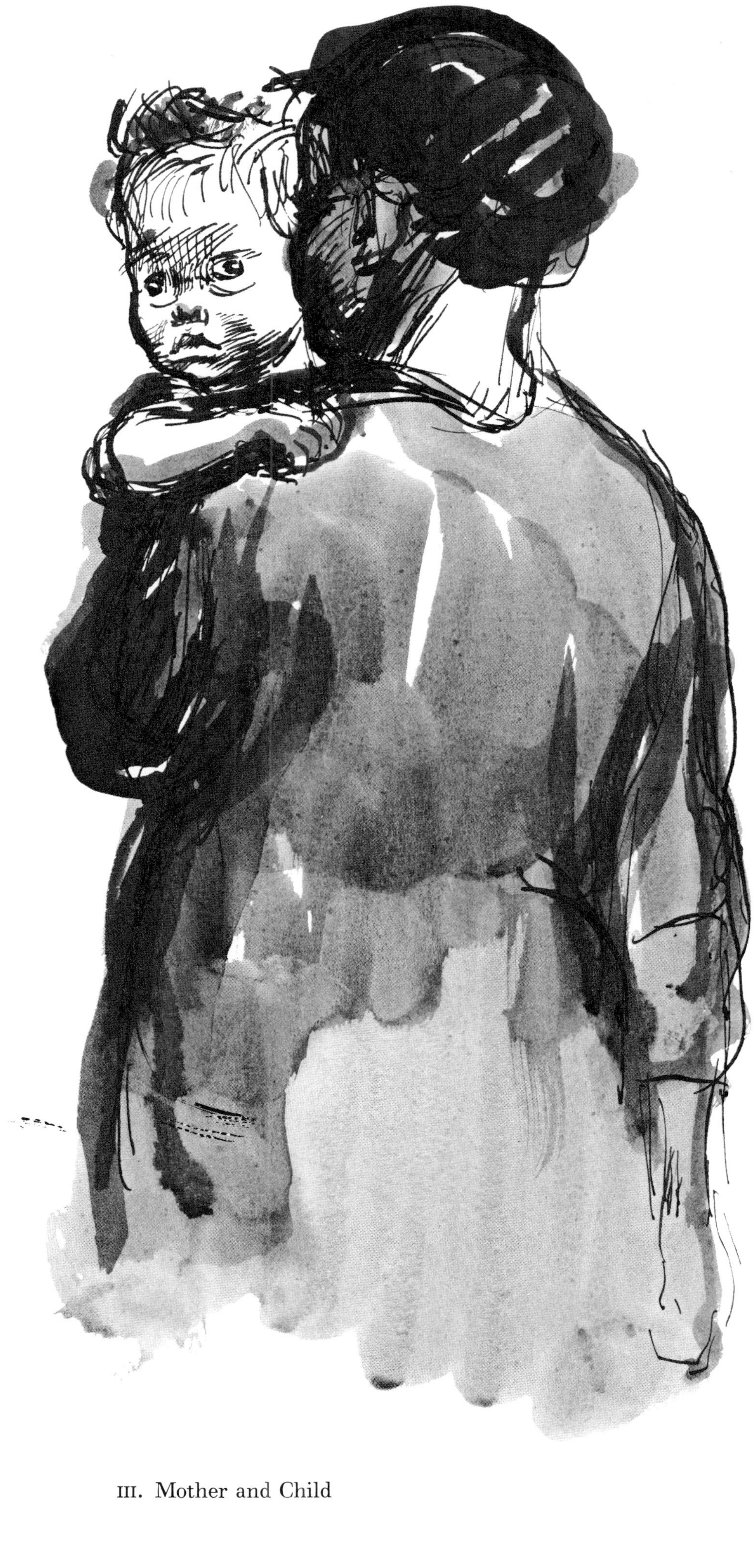

III. Mother and Child

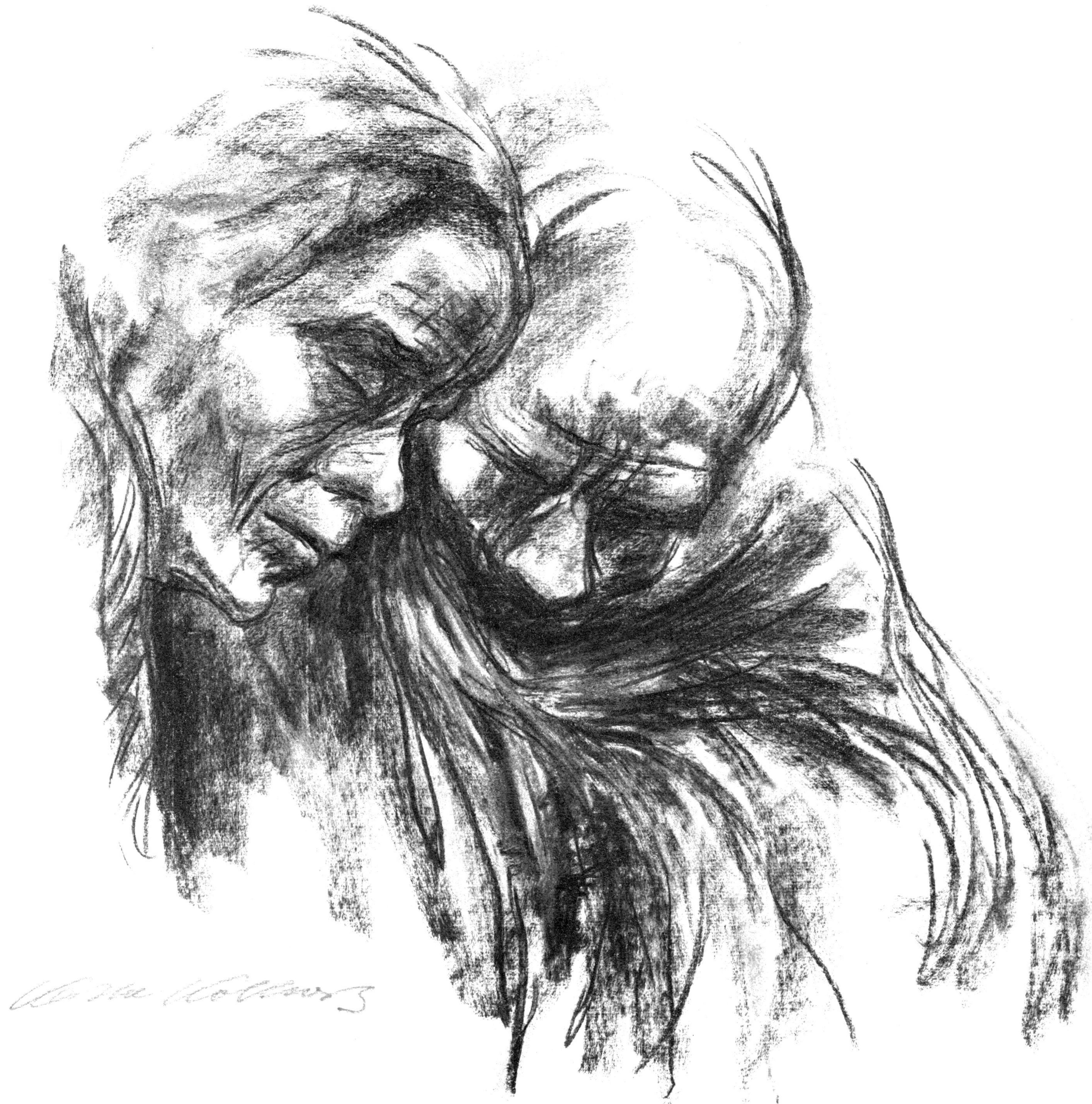

IV. Old Couple

the human race, link between past and future. In the person of the mother, the artist voiced her faith that the people will carry on. In Carl Sandburg's words: *

The learning and blundering people will live on.
They will be tricked and sold and again sold
And go back to the nourishing earth for rootholds,
The people so peculiar in renewal and comeback,
You can't laugh off their capacity to take it.

Two other woodcuts deserve mention. One is *Death with Woman in Lap* of 1921 (Plate 30), serenely beautiful in its balance of light and dark values, in its linear equilibrium. The theme with its gentle intimation of surcease was one that she had attempted many times before, but never so successfully as in this. She was to repeat her success in two later variants, in the bronze memorial plaque of 1935, and in the lithograph of her final cycle (Plate 69). The other block represents her sole venture into a biblical theme, the *Mary and Elizabeth* of 1928 (Plate 31). The story of the Visitation gave scope on the human side to the expression of tender camaraderie in the meeting of the two expectant mothers. It is one of the sweetest and loveliest of her prints without a hint of tragic implication.

During this period, too, she made various other lithographs, emphasizing human rather than social values, intimate glimpses into the daily life of the people. One of the most touching in its expression of parental tenderness was the *Visit to the Children's Hospital* of 1926 (Plate 53). There sits the child, appealing in its unfledged helplessness, whom the mother with maternal practicality is inducing to drink from a cup. The father, equally solicitous but more awkward of ministration, gazes with loving concern upon his offspring. The emotional overtones are suggested with a magic that has seldom been surpassed. In happier vein are the drawing *Woman with Child in Lap* (Plate 1), a strongly plastic conception of 1916, and the lithographs *Boy with Arms around Mother's Neck* (Plate 62), and *Mother with Child in Arms* (Plate 27). Other glimpses of the joys and sorrows of everyday life are *Women Chatting* of 1930 (Plate 63), the poster for the utilization of surplus mother's milk (K.222), and such sketches as *At the Children's Doctor*, based no doubt on observations in her husband's waiting room and afterwards utilized in a poster (K.149). Two lithographs, both depicting listeners, were nevertheless widely divergent in setting: *Prisoners Listening to Music* (K.203, 1925) and *Listeners* (K.228, 1927). The latter, a sympathetic rendering of a father, mother, and child, was based on a sketch made at a celebration in Moscow of the tenth anniversary of the Soviet Union. Along with several other artists and writers she had been invited to Russia for the occasion. Two other expressions of her interest in the Russian people were a poster for Russian relief in 1921 (K.154) and a very large lithograph, also conceived as a poster, *Solidarity: The Propeller Song* (Plate 60). Of this last she wrote, "It was made in the spring of 1932 prompted by a request from Russian artists. In order to make my position clear regarding an imperialistic war against Russia, I drew this lithograph with the inscription *We Protect the Soviet Union* (Propeller Song)." In these later years much of her work has its genesis in some outside request or commission, a poster for some cause she believed in, requests for prints to be issued as membership premiums for various societies, illustrations to works by Romain Rolland, Barbusse, Arno Holz and others. There was no longer the irrepressible urge to self-expression for its own sake; its flow was stimulated only on occasion by external demand.

In 1933 Hitler and the Nazi party came into power. In the purge of radical sympathizers in the fields of art as well as politics, Käthe Kollwitz was expelled from the Berlin Academy of Art, though not otherwise molested. Succeeding years brought anguish of mind and increasing restrictions but never actual imprisonment. Official notices forbidding all commerce in works by interdicted artists were sent to all dealers. This intimidated most of them, but pictures were occasionally bought and sold *sub rosa* or sent out of the country. It seems, therefore, that she was more or less left to her own devices. To be sure, she was not Jewish, though sufficiently identified with the social democrats (majority socialists) and communists by

* From *The People Yes* by courtesy of the publisher, Harcourt Brace and Company.

sympathy and family ties, but not by actual membership or party activities, to have been marked for active persecution. The Nazis no doubt ignored a number of artists, such as Hofer or Sintenis, who, though anti-Nazi in feeling, took no active part in politics; they were after other game. There were also enough other artists, without scruple or principle, willing to minister to the vanity of the ruling ruffians.

About 1938–1939 Erich Cohn of New York offered to get Käthe Kollwitz out of Germany by providing passports and necessary guarantees. She was grateful for his offer but felt she owed it to her family to stay in Germany. She was afraid that if she left the country some anti-Nazi demonstration might be made for her or in her name, which might bring vengeance on her family. So she decided to stick it out in Germany. After all, she was used to neglect and suppression. In the days of the First Reich, the Emperor had forbidden her the gold medal, the Empress had prohibited her poster for an exhibition of *Home Industries* (K.93), and the police had suppressed her poster for a conference on housing and playgrounds, *Greater Berlin* (K.119), as an incitement to class hatred. She had no desire for official patronage, nor did she need it.

This sense of constraint and isolation did, however, have some effect on her; it directed her thoughts and feelings more than ever to the eternal verities. During 1934 and 1935 she worked on her last great print sequence. Once again, it was the fruition of a long period of gestation and travail. The impact of death had long occupied her thought and haunted her imagination. Since 1903 she had made no less than fifteen variants of the subject (K.70, 71, Plate 14, Plate 23, K.113, 114, 115, 116, 117, 118, 129, 140, 151, 187, 188), not to mention related themes in the great cycles and in countless drawings. The set of eight large lithographs has been given several titles. One is Death and Departure (Abschied und Tod) from the portfolio of that name (1924) containing facsimiles of drawings, some of which were prototypes of the lithographs. The artist herself referred to it as the Print-sequence on the Theme of Death (Blätterzug Thema Tod). In Dr. August Klipstein's definitive catalogue of her work the title appears as Death (Vom Tode). It is in reality a procession or dance of death in the grand tradition—visions of death violent and death serene. The conception is lofty though harrowing. She had passed beyond temporal and local attachments and attained an almost godlike understanding and compassion. The prints (Plates 68–75) have no definite order; each is a theme of the same requiem—the drudge of a girl, unlovely in death as in life, at last attaining peace in the lap of death; the man who greats death as an old friend with a hysterical mixture of joy and terror; the mother reaching out her hand to welcome death with resignation in her eyes, contrasting with the horror in those of her child. Finally *The Call of Death* for the one who saw all these visions, her last testament, her swan song, her hail and farewell. There is an amazing immediacy of expression in these prints, sometimes with slashing boldness and vigor, sometimes with tender delicacy, and no concern for niceties of composition or technique. Never have prints carried a greater emotional impact. After 1935 she made only four more prints, notably the pathetic *Self Portrait* of 1938 (Plate 66) and the vigorous *Seed Corn Must Not Be Ground* of 1942 (Plate 64), a protest against the recruiting of young boys into the army.

In the later years she worked much on sculpture. In August 1939 she wrote to Erich Cohn: "My work, alas often interrupted, consists almost exclusively of small sculptures. In the beginning it was hard for me to turn from the larger format to the smaller. This is particularly noticeable in the groups *Women Waving Goodbye* and *Women Protecting Their Children*. The group, *Pietà*, is somewhat larger in size so that I could rest my eyes. Now, I am much interested in these smaller works. I am fortunate that I can still work, even though, as I have said, under difficulties and handicaps."

Her husband died in 1940. For the last year of her life she lived at the Moritzburg as a guest of Ernst Heinrich, Prince of Saxony. This castle, the hereditary seat of a branch of the former royal Saxon line, is situated just north of Dresden, and contains a fine collection of porcelain and graphic arts as well as a big library. Some of Käthe Kollwitz's very latest work is to be found in the Moritzburg. According to Dr. August

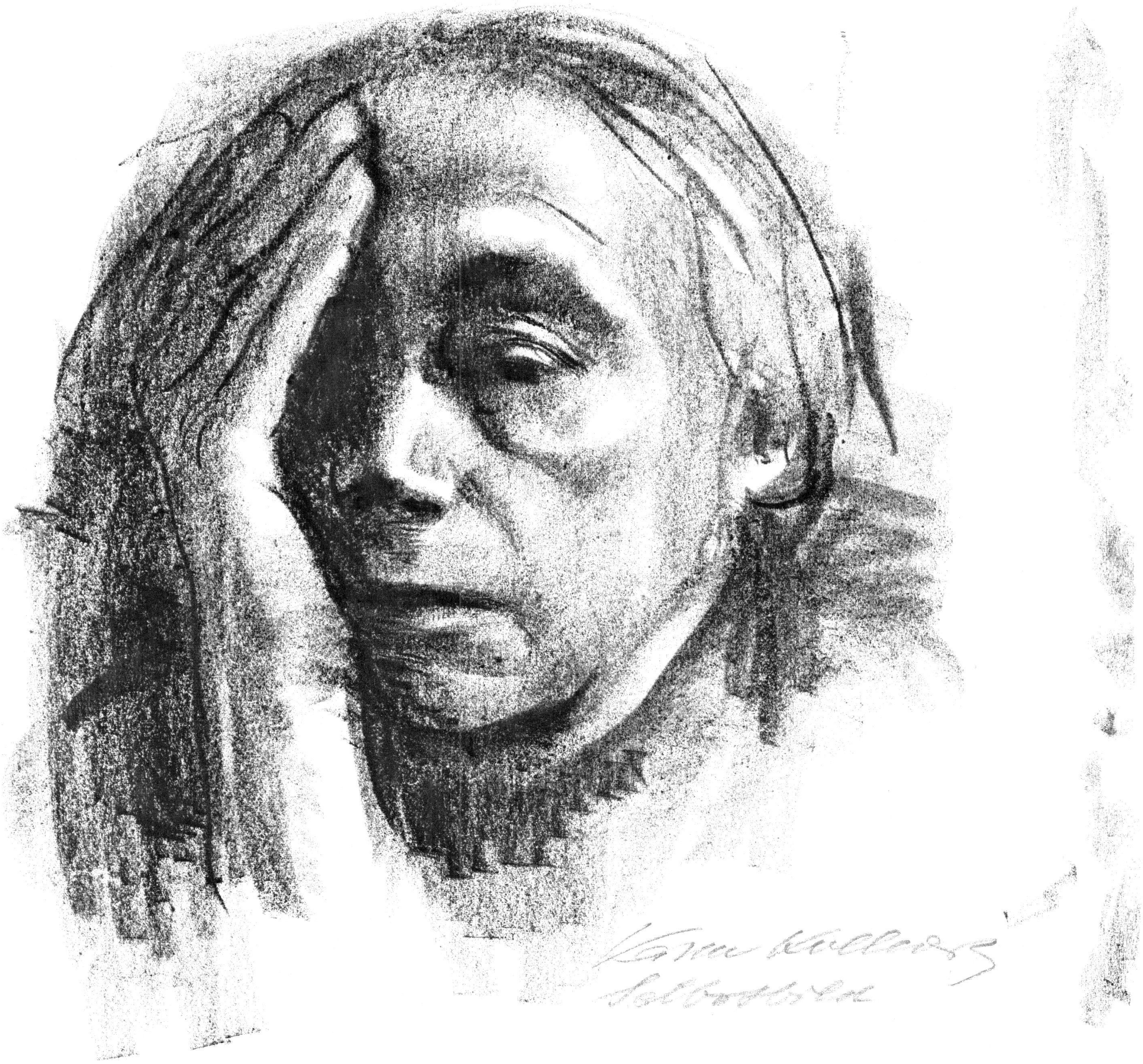

v. Self Portrait, 1925

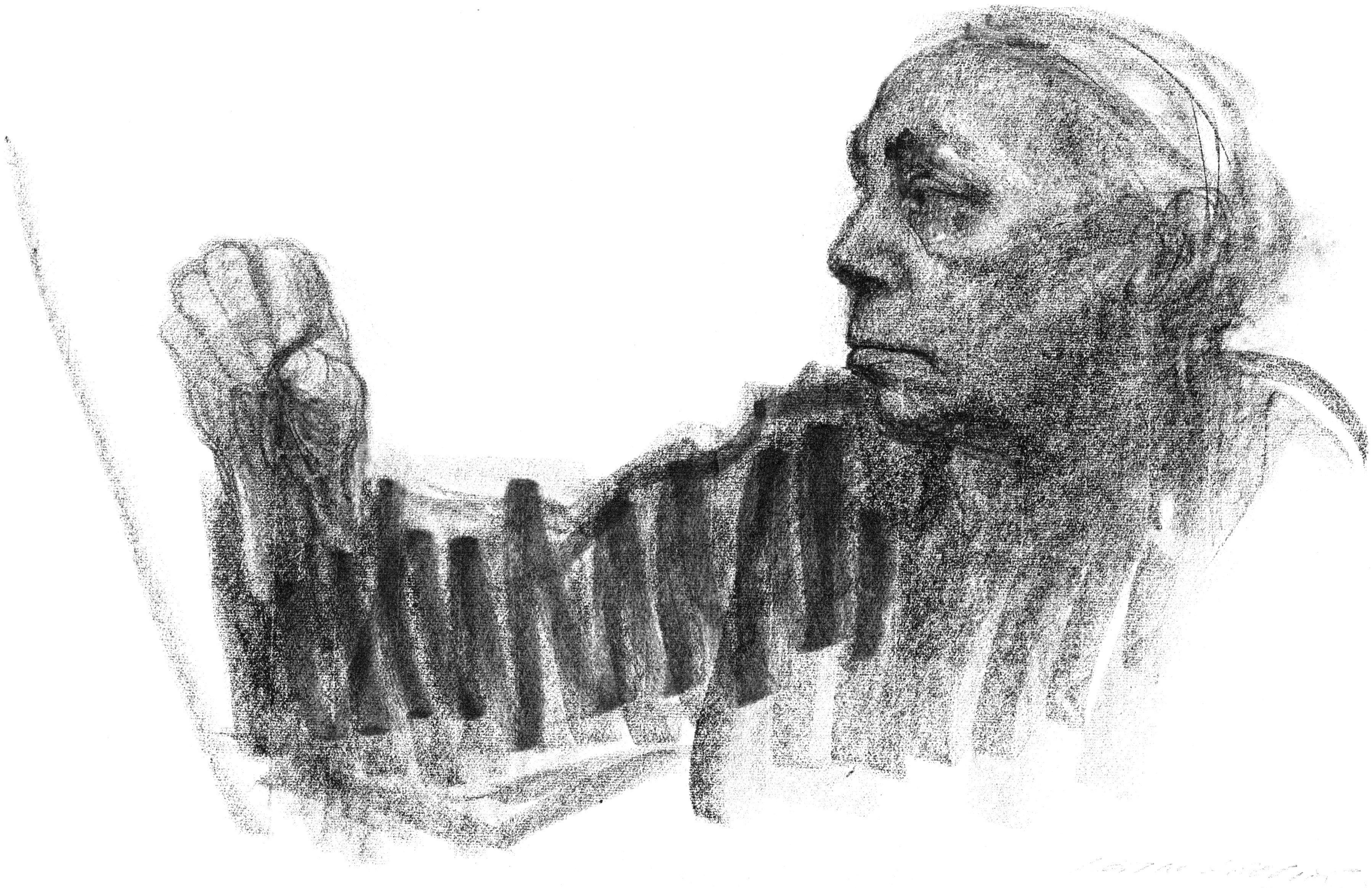

VI. Self Portrait, 1933

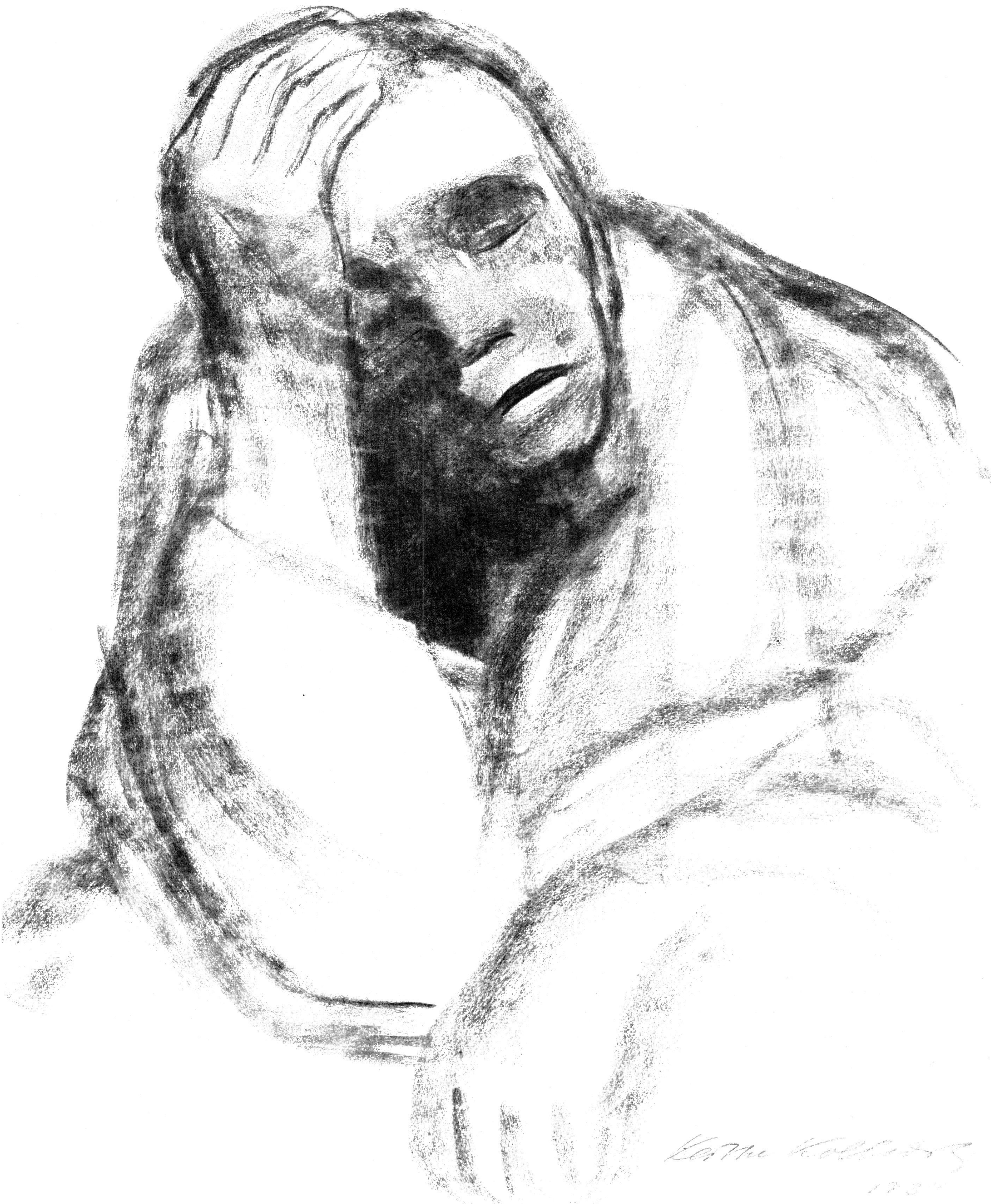

VII. Self Portrait, 1934

Klipstein, her old house in Berlin was bombed out, and with it her complete print collection, comprising many unique trials and unpublished proofs, as well as many drawings. A portfolio she had taken with her alone survived. This contained drawings she especially prized for their association with her home and family. Käthe Kollwitz died on April 22, 1945. She was cremated in Meissen, and her ashes were brought to Berlin (Friederichsfelde). Karl Buchholz, who saw her but a few months before her death, had the feeling that she was living in a bright and serene inner world, more and more withdrawn even from her own art and work.

From her numerous self portraits—she made at least fifty in prints, drawings, and sculpture—one gets some idea of how she looked (Frontispiece, Plates V–VII, 2, 40–43, 65, 66). She made practically no other portraits, which is natural in one whose expression was so strongly colored by her own inner experience. In a sense one might say that her whole work was a self portrait. From those so labeled, one can follow the traces left by time and experience over the years, from the rounded freshness of the young bride to the lined and seared face of the aged woman. These records do not stem from a superficial narcissism but from frank self appraisal: they are psychological milestones. George Grosz has a vivid recollection of her: "I met her only once, at a reception of the Berlin Academy where she was a member (Liebermann was president then, before Hitler came in). . . . Somebody introduced me to her. But we exchanged only a few polite phrases; I had the feeling she didn't belong among such a festive and rather social crowd. I think she kept quite to herself. . . . She had white hair then —a certain aura of melancholy was about her—far from talkative, rather moody." Dr. W. R. Valentiner also remembers seeing her at a meeting of artists in the revolutionary days of 1919, "following the discussion intently but never saying a word."

Thus she was in public, shy and retiring. Others have testified that in more intimate surroundings she was natural and outgoing, a human being who could laugh and dance and sing on occasion, but whose outlook in general was grave and methodical. Since her mind worked rather slowly, what she said was never brilliant, but it always carried weight and conviction. At her home there might be long discussions on socialism, philosophy, religion, or psychology, as well as frequent reading aloud from books. She has testified on several occasions how much Goethe meant to her. She liked to go to the theater and to concerts and never missed a performance of Bach's *St. Matthew Passion* or Beethoven's Ninth Symphony. The Kollwitz family loved to wander on foot and often spent their whole vacation in that way. Sunday excursions to the countryside around Berlin were fairly customary.

From her letters and other sources one can get a further sense of her personality: the simplicity of her dress, the quiet dignity of her bearing, her distaste for personal aggrandizement of any kind. She masked her reticence and sense of privacy in a certain formality of manner. Louise Diehl has spoken of this aloofness; there were certain idly curious questions one dared not ask about her work. The feeling for privacy appears also in her scruples regarding the publication of a drawing she made of Barlach on his deathbed (letter to Curt Valentin, January 30, 1940): "I consider it almost an indiscretion to make it public when I think of Barlach's retiring disposition. He would not have favored it, and I shall therefore make the photograph accessible only to the circle of his closest friends. The drawing itself will go to Güstrow, where it is hoped his work will be assembled. Thereby your question whether I would make a lithograph of the same subject is also answered."

She was not grasping in her business dealings, but she respected her own work and her mission as an artist. There were certain things she would not sell at any price, especially after she had learned her lesson during the inflation period. Like any artist absorbed in self expression she showed a keen interest in everything related to her work and its reception by the general public. Though she was self centered in her art, she could appreciate other people's work. Curt Valentin recalls seeing her often—indeed oftener than any other Berlin artist—at the Flechtheim Gallery.

Käthe Kollwitz was on the whole a sound critic of her own work. Her judgment of her best subjects coincides fairly well with the critical consensus.

The selection of plates in *Das Kollwitz Werk* of 1930 is supposed to have been her own. A list she compiled of the prints she particularly valued (à propos an exhibition to travel around the United States, in a letter to Erich Cohn, August 10, 1938) is also so enlightening that it is here published in full:

ETCHINGS

Weavers cycle complete, Plates 3–8
Uprising, Plate 9
La Carmagnole, Plate 10
Peasant War cycle complete, Plates 15–21
Mother with Dead Child, Plate 14
Unemployed, K.100
Woman and Death, Plate 23
Run Over, Plate 25
Mother with Child in Arms, Plate 26
Self Portrait, Plate 40

LITHOGRAPHS

Mother with Child in Arms, Plate 27
Mothers, Plate 28
Woman Reflecting, Plate 44
Bread!, Plate 49
Self Portrait 1924, K.198
Home Industry, K.209
Visit to the Children's Hospital, Plate 53
Municipal Lodging, Plate 54
Woman with Sleeping Child, Plate 61
Self Portrait 1934, Plate 43
Death cycle complete, Plates 68–75

WOODCUTS

War cycle complete, Plates 32–38
Proletariat cycle complete, K.206, 207, Plate 56

I have already spoken of what might be called her artistic conscience, the way she labored for the perfection of her expression and particularly for the definitive rendering of her conception. There were, to cite but one example, four completed variants (K.22, 23, 26, 31) of *Poverty* in the Weavers cycle before she decided on the fifth and final version (Plate 3). Variants of many other subjects exist and no doubt many others were destroyed. Countless drawings were made as studies for prints, compositional sketches, studies of details, arms, heads, figures, and the like. Again, the number of stages or "states" (in some instances as many as nine) through which certain plates and blocks passed, bears witness to her industry and patience. A letter she wrote to Erich Cohn in May 1938 throws light on this: "Naturally I cut my own wood blocks. It is only through the difficulties which ensue in the cutting and in their more or less successful solution, that the work becomes interesting. It has happened on various occasions that I have hopelessly spoiled a particular section on the block, and then had to send it to a shop to be corrected. This is done by cutting out the bad spot and inserting a new piece of wood in the hole. A similar method exists for an etching. The spoiled section on the copper is hammered up from the rear and the bulge ground down till it is level with the rest of the plate. In both instances a brand new surface is provided on the block or plate, which can then be reworked. Also there can be various states in a wood block just as in a copper plate, though hardly so many."

Mention has also been made of her expert technical manipulation. She experimented with many complex graphic mediums, particularly in intaglio and lithography and their combinations. There was masterly use of crayon work, pen work, tusche wash, and scratching on the stone of *Death* (Plate 4) of the Weavers cycle. There were combinations of etching and lithography (K.54, 56). Straight etching, associated with soft-ground, was much employed in the Peasant War cycle; *Outbreak* (Plate 19) in addition had aquatint, pen-and-ink-wash-out-etching (*Aussprengverfahren*) and several varieties of textile textures (through a soft-ground). It is interesting to note that this plate, in spite of its elaboration of technique, is one of the most dynamic in feeling and composition. In *Woman and Death* (Plate 23), carborundum soft-ground (*Schmirgeldurchdruck* or what in English is generally called sandpaper aquatint) was used in conjunction with straight etching. At times she employed still other mediums, such as aquatint, burin engraving, drypoint, and several kinds of soft-ground. In lithography she worked on stone, aluminum plates, as well as on a variety of transfer papers. Many of the later lithographs were transfers. This technical virtuosity always remained a means to an end; it was never displayed for its own sake. With her, content was always of prime importance. There is a phrase which she used more than once to describe her work. The simile possibly came from chemistry. It is so apt and descriptive of her creative approach that it is worth quoting: such and such a print was a "precipitate of impressions" (*Niederschlag von Eindrücken*) gathered at such and such a time.

The work of Käthe Kollwitz has been dismissed by some critics as merely propaganda. The term, especially in the antinomy of art versus propaganda, is often loosely used. In a sense all religious art is propaganda—art in the service of religion—yet no discredit is attached to it as such. Posters and advertising in general can be called propaganda, yet a poster by Toulouse-Lautrec is none the less a work of art. In political cartooning it is harder to draw the line. It is the cartoonist's job to dramatize the tactical exigencies of the party line from day to day; he must be partisan and tough on opponents with no concession to integrity or tolerant understanding. Yet Daumier has been acclaimed a great artist. Again, if an artist feels strongly about some issue or situation, as Callot or Goya did about war for example, their print message is not automatically excluded from the status of art. Propaganda, then, is special pleading of a sort. It can be ephemeral or enduring. If it is ephemeral, it will be out of date when political tactics are realigned or when the issue is trivial or partisan; it will be unconvincing when the motivation is half-baked and the idea not cast in terms of creative expression. It will be a work of art only if its appeal is enduring, if the artist speaks purely in terms of his art, if his allegiance is not to party but to humanity, if the issues are the eternal verities—death, suffering, love, children.

There are less than a score of posters by Käthe Kollwitz, frankly and efficiently posters: appeals on behalf of starving children, for playgrounds and better housing, for exhibitions of women's home industries, for relief in Austria and Russia, against war, against loan sharks and drunkenness. That is special pleading but not specious pleading. She was not political minded. She said she knew no party, only brothers; and it is manifest in all her work. Her maternal sympathy could not encompass hate or triviality. Satire was beyond her. It was man's role to attack or to fight. Woman-like, she observed compassionately, or she bound up the wounds and celebrated the martyrs as in *Karl Liebknecht Memorial*, and the Weavers and Peasant War cycles. She pleaded for solidarity in *Propeller Song* or fraternization in the lithograph of that name. The bulk of her work consisted of worker's types, some men, but chiefly women and children. She delineated to the best of her ability but dragged in no moral. Social conditions were the stuff of her art. She had the gift of generalizing from the particular into the universal, of creating types. What Millet did with the peasant, she did with the worker—projected a way of life, envisaged a noble world. An ideal world, to be sure, not the whole story, not realistic, as George Grosz once said, the vulgarity, the shoddiness, the dregs of city life were left out. It was pure as Rembrandt's world was pure, and realistic too, in a way: psychologically real, psychologically true. Emotions are timeless and do not change.

The question of proletarian art also needs clarification. Can there be a real portrait of the worker? Who is the proletarian, the peasant, the bourgeois, the capitalist, or the aborigine? They are all human beings of infinite shading and variety. No one can give a complete picture of all or even of any one category. It is necessary at times to interpret them in terms of a certain function. This can be done more efficiently and with less distortion, scientifically, statistically as in calculus. In art there is a similar generalized interpretation, just as abstract as the terms in calculus, namely the symbol that has power to sway the emotions. Käthe Kollwitz has created symbols of this kind. How successful they are may be judged by comparing them with the work of a contemporary and equally socially conscious artist, such as Steinlen. With few exceptions his work "dates," for it is too specifically illustrative. It has not her universal validity nor her emotional impact. Käthe Kollwitz has made a noble contribution to the mythology of the working class.

Yet one may question whether that was her sole or ultimate intention. Her role as a dramatic artist has already been emphasized. It is possible to view her work from this angle as an objective study of mass movement and psychology, or of the individual under the stress of emotion. Hemingway in *Death in the Afternoon* has given some inkling of the difficulty the writer experiences in trying to communicate feeling, in building up emotional potential through a recital of ambient details. The artist, like the mime, has a somewhat easier task because he can work through gesture and facial expression (not to mention line and color). Certainly Rembrandt, Goya, and Daumier, to cite but a few, had an uncanny power to suggest emotional overtones. Käthe Kollwitz had a similar power, and her work might easily serve as a sourcebook of gesture and behavior. We can see how a wife acts when she gets the news that her husband has been killed, how it feels to beg with desperation, in what diverse ways parents love their children, how crowds act when driven to frenzy, how people act when drunk or when there is an accident. The repertoire is weighted on the sombre side, but then, as Hemingway points out, there is no better catalyst than violent death to precipitate a pure emotion. One is convinced that the reactions of her characters are innately felt and psychologically true, hardly ever melodramatic or exaggerated. The reason for this, one almost believes, is that she tested them on herself. In a letter to Arthur Bonus she recalled a story which bears witness to this: "When Peter was seven years old and I was working on the etching *Mother with Dead Child* [Plate 14], I made sketches in the mirror of myself holding him in my arms. It was very exhausting and I let out a groan. Then his childish voice piped up to comfort me: 'Never mind, Mother, it will be beautiful.'"

What was the ultimate drive that carried her on through seventy-eight years of creative life? It was, in my opinion, a moral or philosophic imperative. Like most of the socially conscious artists of her time, she lived in a world of conflicting social patterns and of individual reactions to them. The ethic of her social conscience was a personal evaluation of right and wrong and not a tactic of organized mass movements, it was social justice and not the economic interpretation of history. However much she might understand and sympathize with the revolutionary gesture of the class struggle, it was not her motivation. Her grandfather spoke in her more strongly than she knew. Her Christian background was modified by ideas of economic materialism and emerged as a tragic outlook on life. The sense of suffering humanity remained and found utterance through her talent as a dramatic artist. It was almost a Buddhistic conception, life as a vale of tears, a tragic error, a futile involvement in the wheel of causation with its never ending round of ignorance and desire and pain. She suffered much and attained a degree of philosophic detachment. From this height she could look on others with understanding and compassion. This attitude, it seems to me, gives special meaning to her last great opus on the theme of Death. It also throws light on the prevailing sombre tone of her whole work. Those who do not possess this detachment find her work gloomy and oppressive. Life is not like that, they say. Life is many things. This was the facet she saw. Temperament and experience impose on every artist the direction of his talents; and we accept this limitation. We do not ask of Michelangelo that he be frivolous or of Fragonard that he be melancholy.

Bibliography

Bittner, Herbert. *Kaethe Kollwitz Drawings.* New York: 1959.

Bonus, Arthur. *Das Kaethe Kollwitz-Werk.* Mit einführendem Text von Arthur Bonus. Dresden: 1925.

Deri, Max. *Sonder-Ausstellung Kaethe Kollwitz zu ihrem 50. Geburtstag, Apr.–Mai, 1917.* Vorwort von Max Deri. Berlin: 1917.

Diel, Louise. *Kaethe Kollwitz; ein Ruf ertönt, eine Einführung in das Lebenswerk der Künstlerin.* Berlin: 1927.

Elias, Julius. "Kaethe Kollwitz," in *Kunst und Künstler*, Vol. XVI, pp. 540–549. Berlin: 1917.

Hartmann, W. G. *(Kaethe Kollwitz) 24 Handzeichnungen in originalgetreuen Wiedergaben.* Mit einem Vorwort von W. G. Hartmann. Dresden: 1920.

Hauptmann, Gerhart. *Abschied und Tod. Acht Zeichnungen von Käthe Kollwitz.* Berlin: 1924.

Heilborn, Adolf. *Die Zeichner des Volkes. Käthe Kollwitz-Heinrich Zille.* Berlin: 1925.

Heilborn, Adolf. *Käthe Kollwitz.* Berlin: 1949 (4th ed.).

Heise, C. G. *Käthe Kollwitz. Einundzwanzig Zeichnungen der späten Jahre.* Berlin: 1948.

Kaemmerer, Ludwig. *(Käthe Kollwitz) Griffelkunst und Weltanschauung. Ein kunstgeschichtlicher Beitrag zur Seelen- und Gesellschaftskunde.* Dresden: 1923.

Klipstein, August. *Käthe Kollwitz; Verzeichnis des graphischen Werkes.* Bern: 1955.

Kollwitz, Kaethe. *Das neue Kollwitz-Werk.* Texte der Künstlerin. Dresden: 1933.

Kollwitz, Kaethe. *Tagebuchblätter und Briefe.* Herausgegeben von Hans Kollwitz. Berlin: 1948.

Kollwitz, Kaethe. *The Diaries and Letters of Kaethe Kollwitz.* Translated by Richard and Clara Winston. Chicago: 1955.

Kollwitz, Kaethe. "Ich will wirken in dieser Zeit," *Auswahl aus den Tagebüchern und Briefen, aus Graphik, Zeichnungen und Plastik.* Einführung von Friedrich Ahlers-Hestermann. Berlin: 1952.

Kollwitz, Kaethe. *Briefe der Freundschaft und Begegnungen.* Mit einem Anhang aus dem Tagebuch von Hans Kollwitz und Berichten über Käthe Kollwitz. Munich: 1966.

Kuhn, Alfred. *Käthe Kollwitz.* Berlin: 1921.

Kurth, Willy. *Käthe Kollwitz. Geleitwort zum Katalog der Käthe Kollwitz-Ausstellung in der Deutschen Akademie der Künste.* Berlin: 1951.

Lehrs, Max. "Käthe Kollwitz," in *Die Graphischen Künste*, Vol. XXVI, pp. 55–67. Vienna: 1910.

McCausland, Elizabeth. *Käthe Kollwitz. Ten Lithographs.* New York: 1941.

Müller, J. "Käthe Kollwitz," in *Allgemeines Lexikon der bildenden Künstler* (Thieme-Becker), Vol. XXI, pp. 245–247. Leipzig: 1927.

Nagel, Otto. *Käthe Kollwitz.* Dresden: 1963.

Nagel, Otto. *Die Selbstbildnisse der Käthe Kollwitz.* Dresden: 1965.

Schmalenbach, Fritz. *Käthe Kollwitz.* Bern: 1948.

Schumann, Werner. *Käthe Kollwitz. Ein Herz schlägt für die Mütter.* 100 Handzeichnungen. Hanover: 1953.

Sievers, Johannes. *Die Radierungen und Steindrucke von Käthe Kollwitz innerhalb der Jahre 1890 bis 1912; ein beschreibendes Verzeichnis.* Dresden: 1913.

Strauss, Gerhard. *Käthe Kollwitz.* Dresden: 1950.

Thiem, Gunther. *Die Zeichnerin Käthe Kollwitz.* Catalogue of the Centennial Exhibition, Staatsgalerie. Stuttgart: 1967.

Von der Becke, A. *(Käthe Kollwitz) Handzeichnungen und graphische Seltenheiten; eine Ausstellung zum 100. Geburtstag.* Munich: A. Von der Becke, 1967?.

Wagner, A. *Die Radierungen, Holzschnitte und Lithographien von Käthe Kollwitz; eine Zusammenstellung der seit 1912 entstandenen graphischen Arbeiten in chronologischer Folge.* Dresden: 1927.

Worringer, Wilhelm. *Käthe Kollwitz.* Königsberg: 1931.

List of Illustrations

The letter K. refers to the definitive catalogue raisonné by August Klipstein, published in 1955
The letter B. refers to Herbert Bittner's monograph on Kollwitz drawings, 1959
Full titles of these works are given in the Bibliography

LIST OF ILLUSTRATIONS

PRINTS AND DRAWINGS OF KÄTHE KOLLWITZ

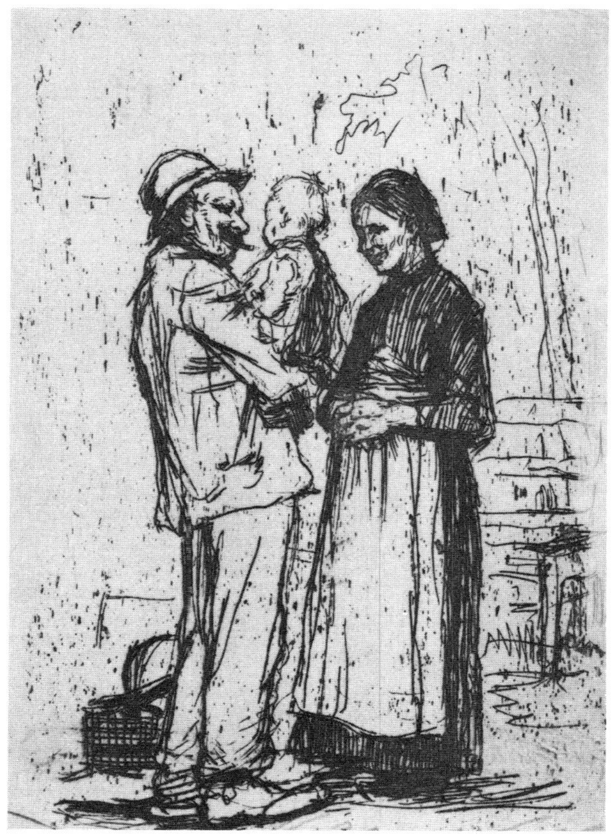

1. Greeting

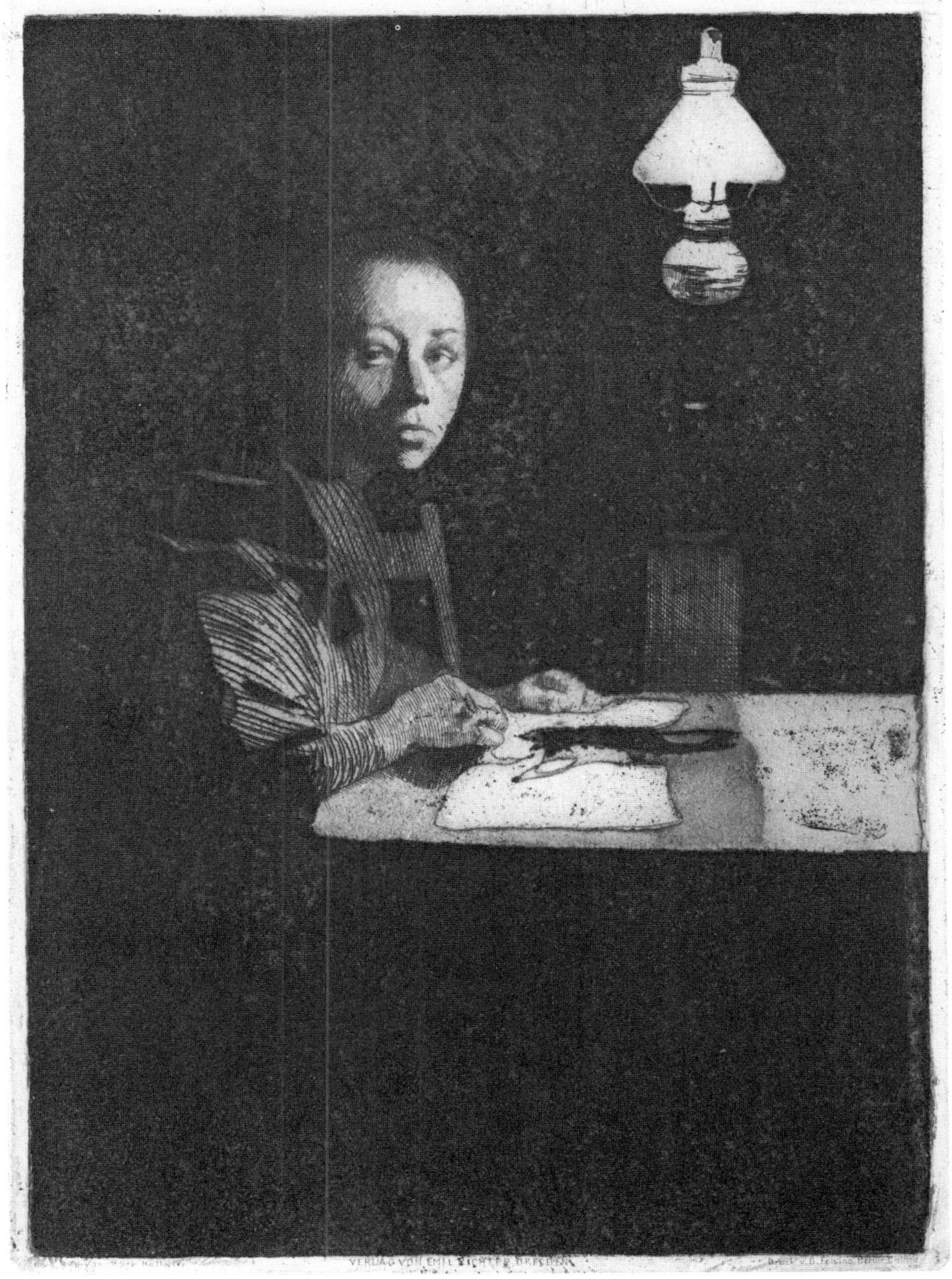

2. Self Portrait at Table, 1893

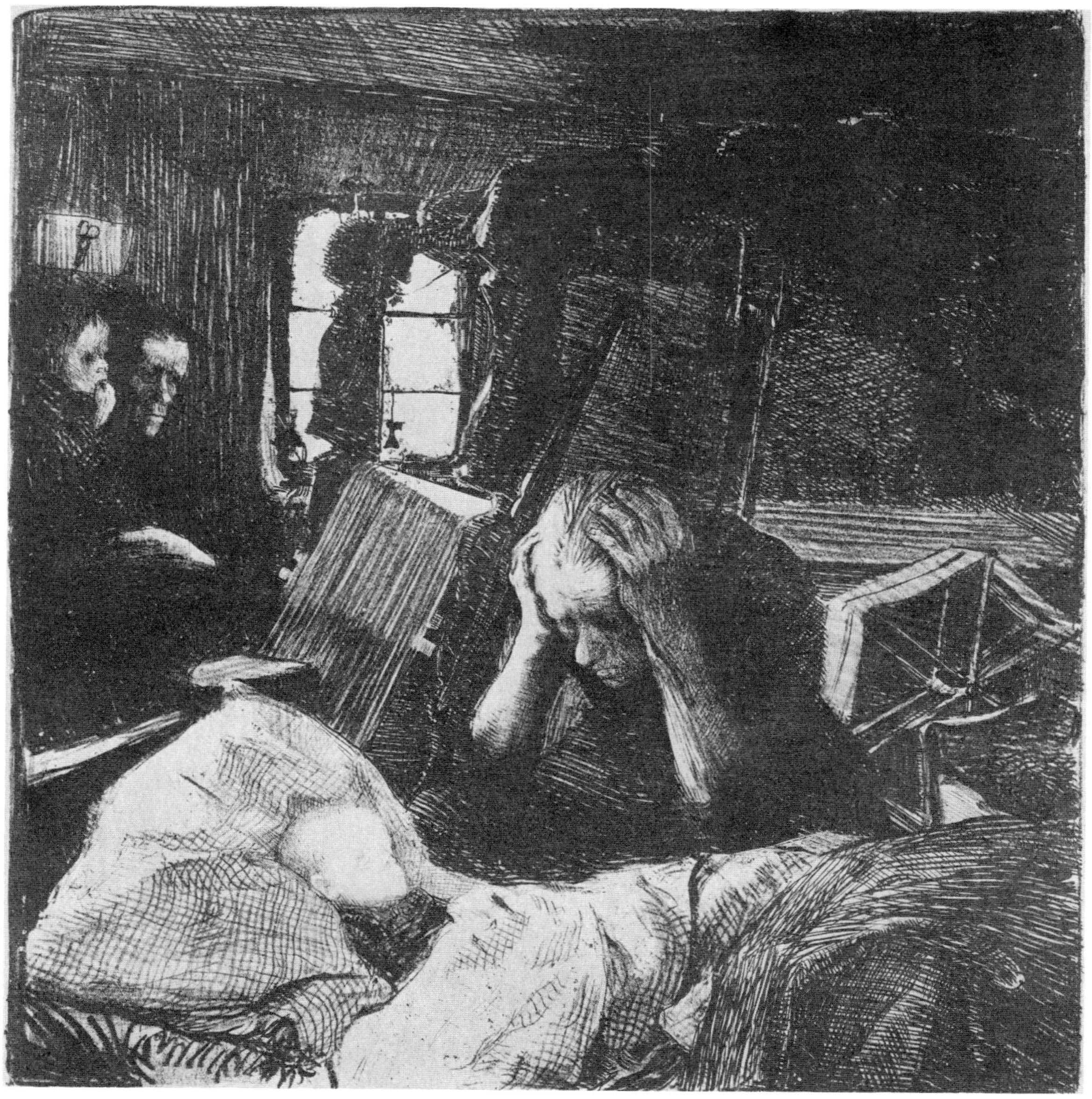

3. Poverty

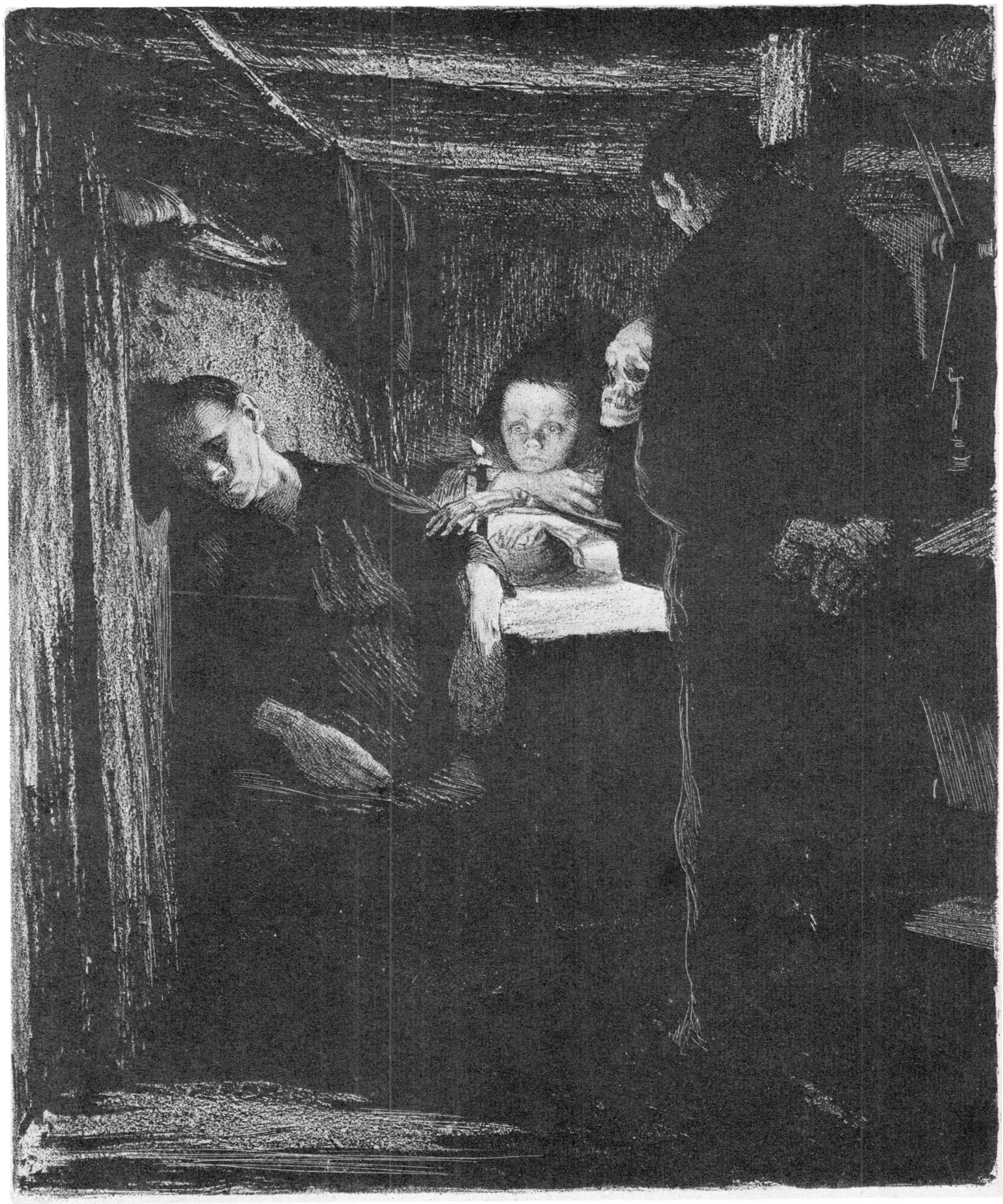

4. Death

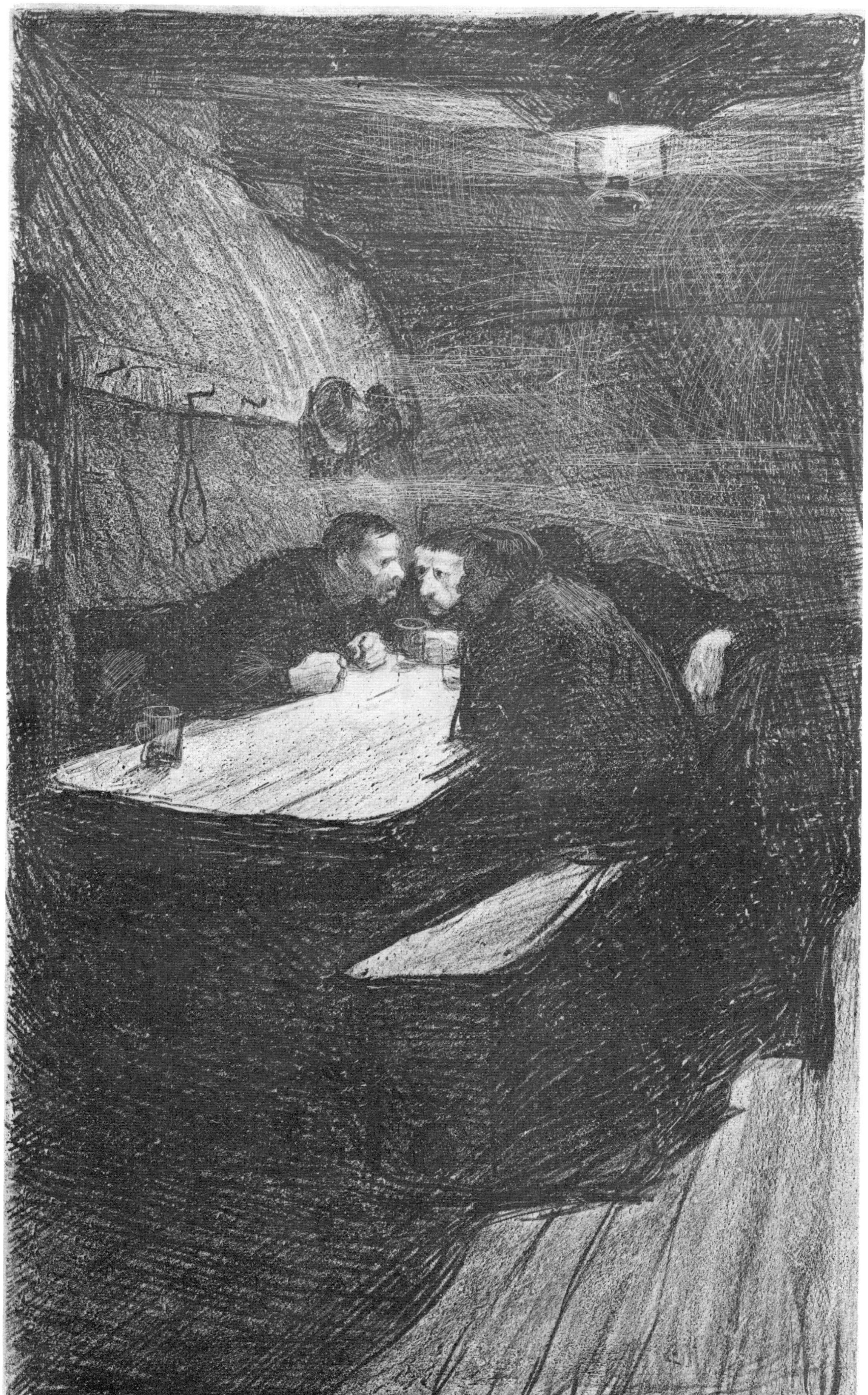

5. Conspiracy

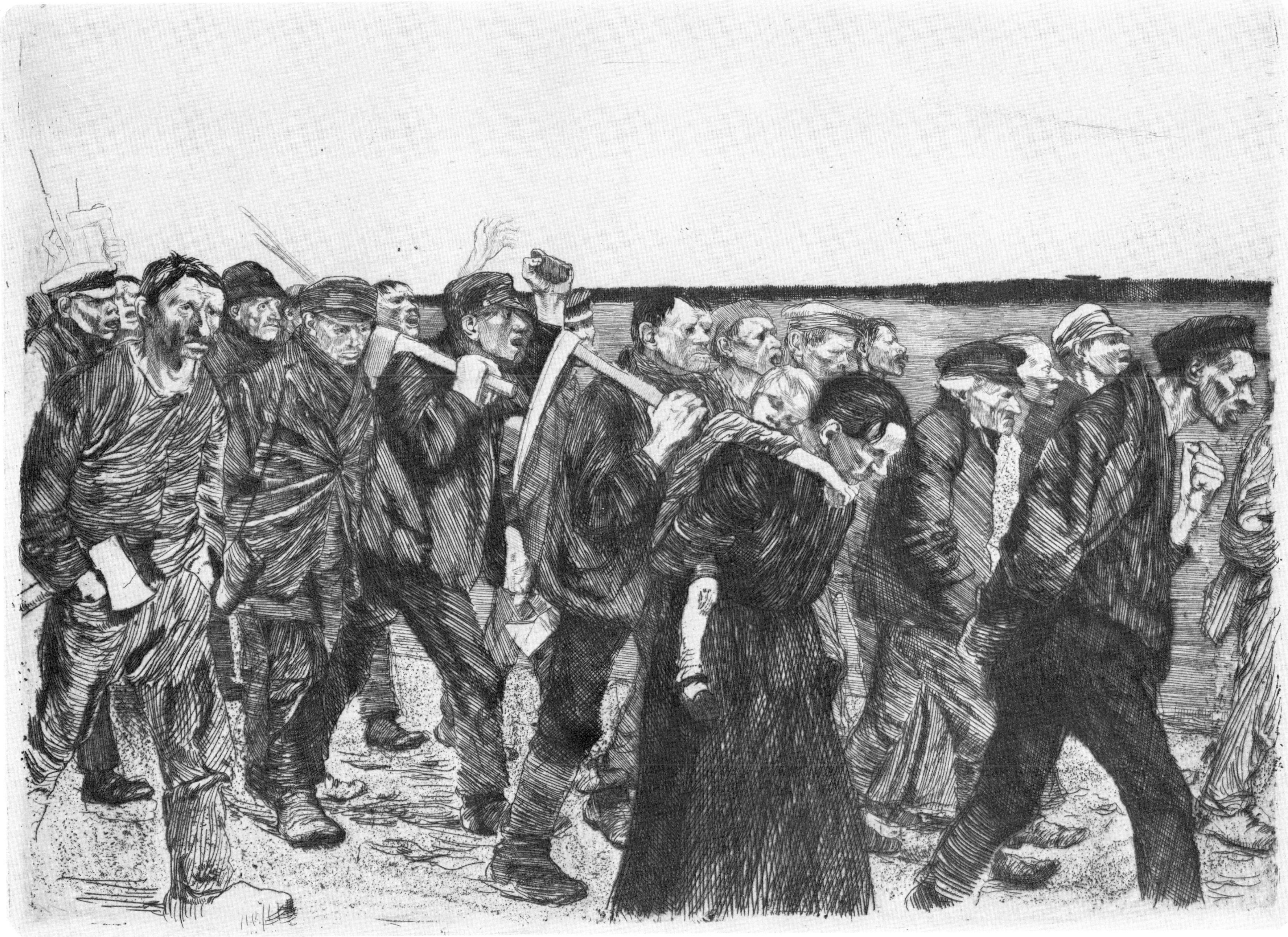

6. March of the Weavers

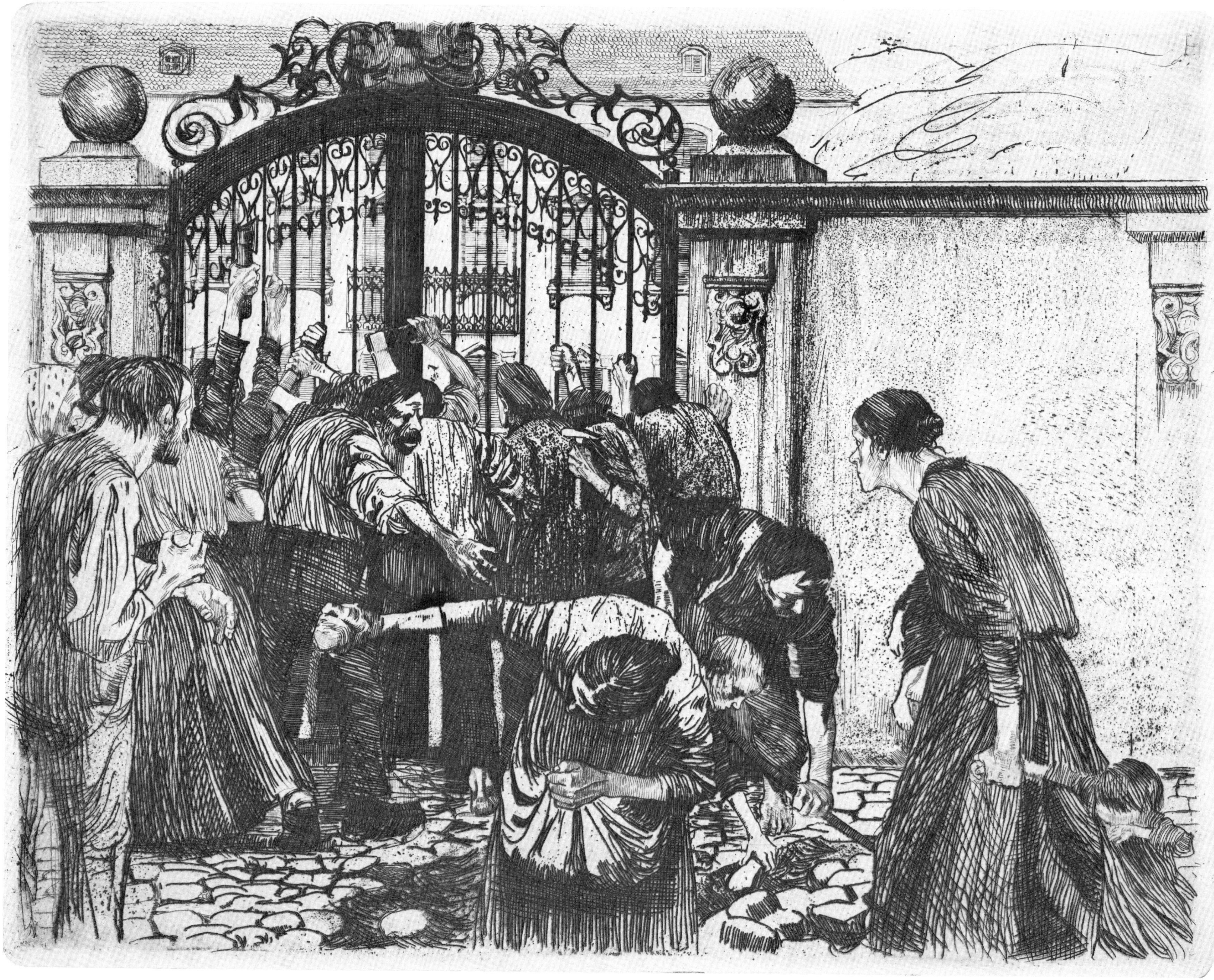

7. Riot

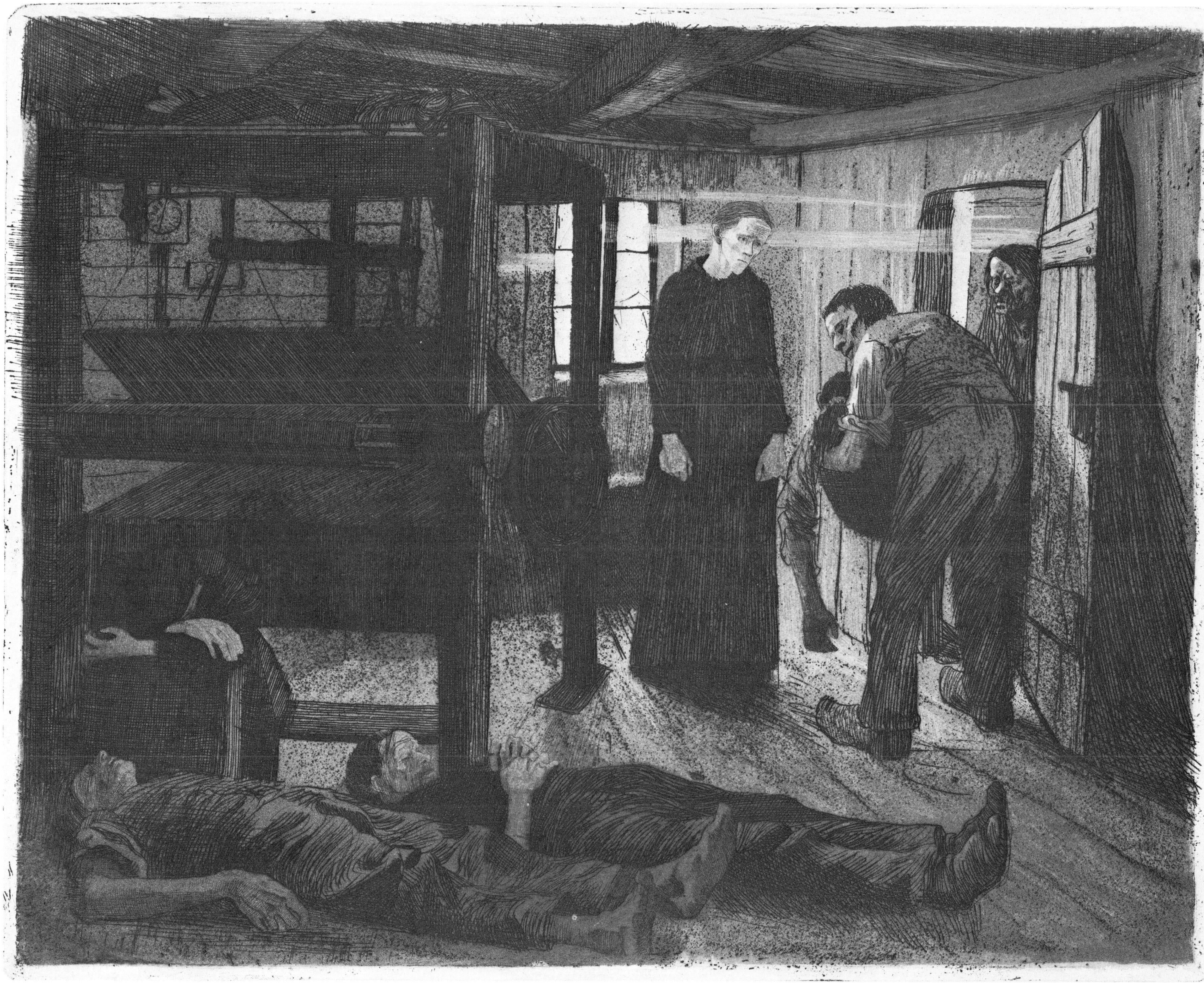

8. The End

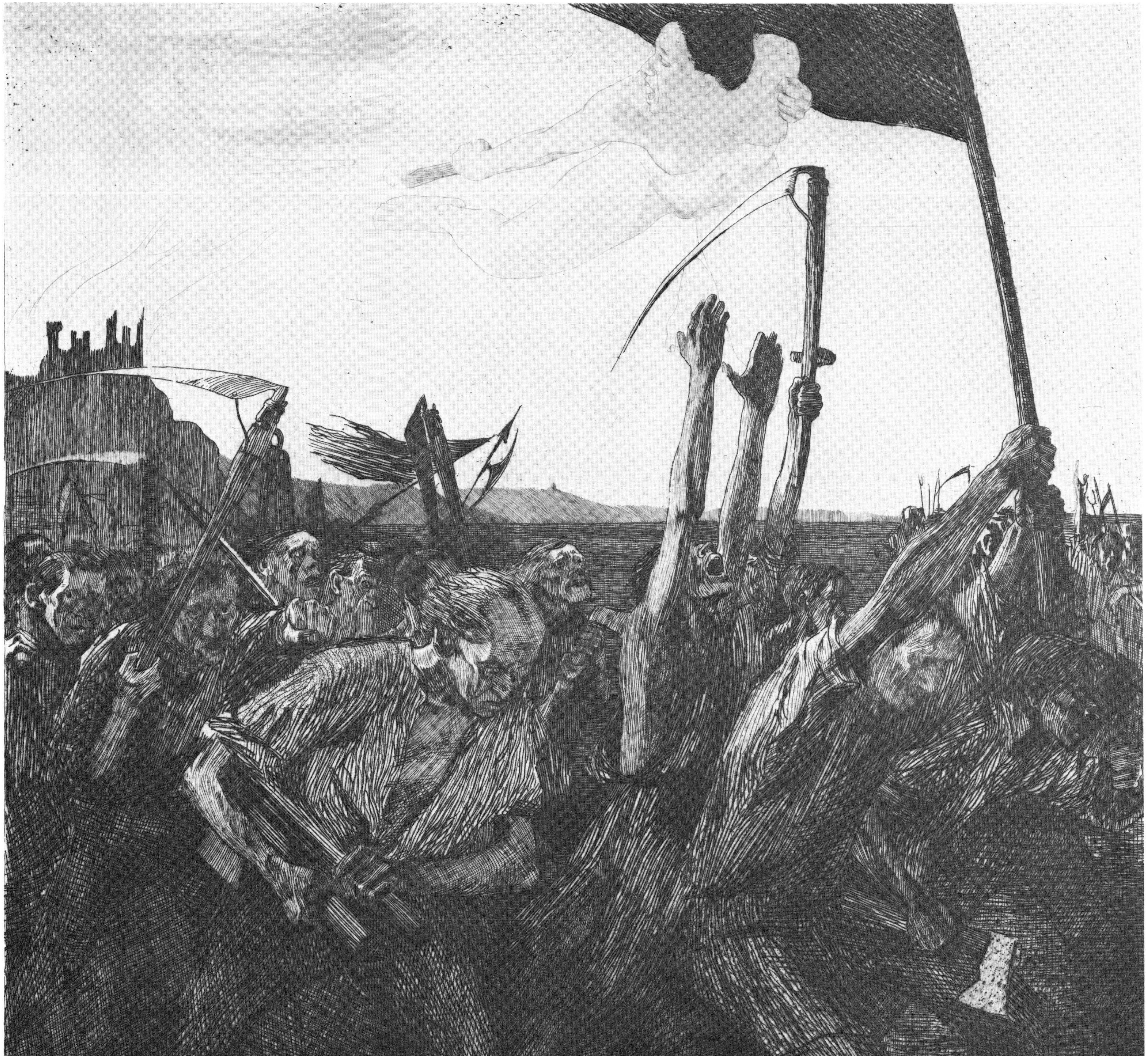

9. Uprising

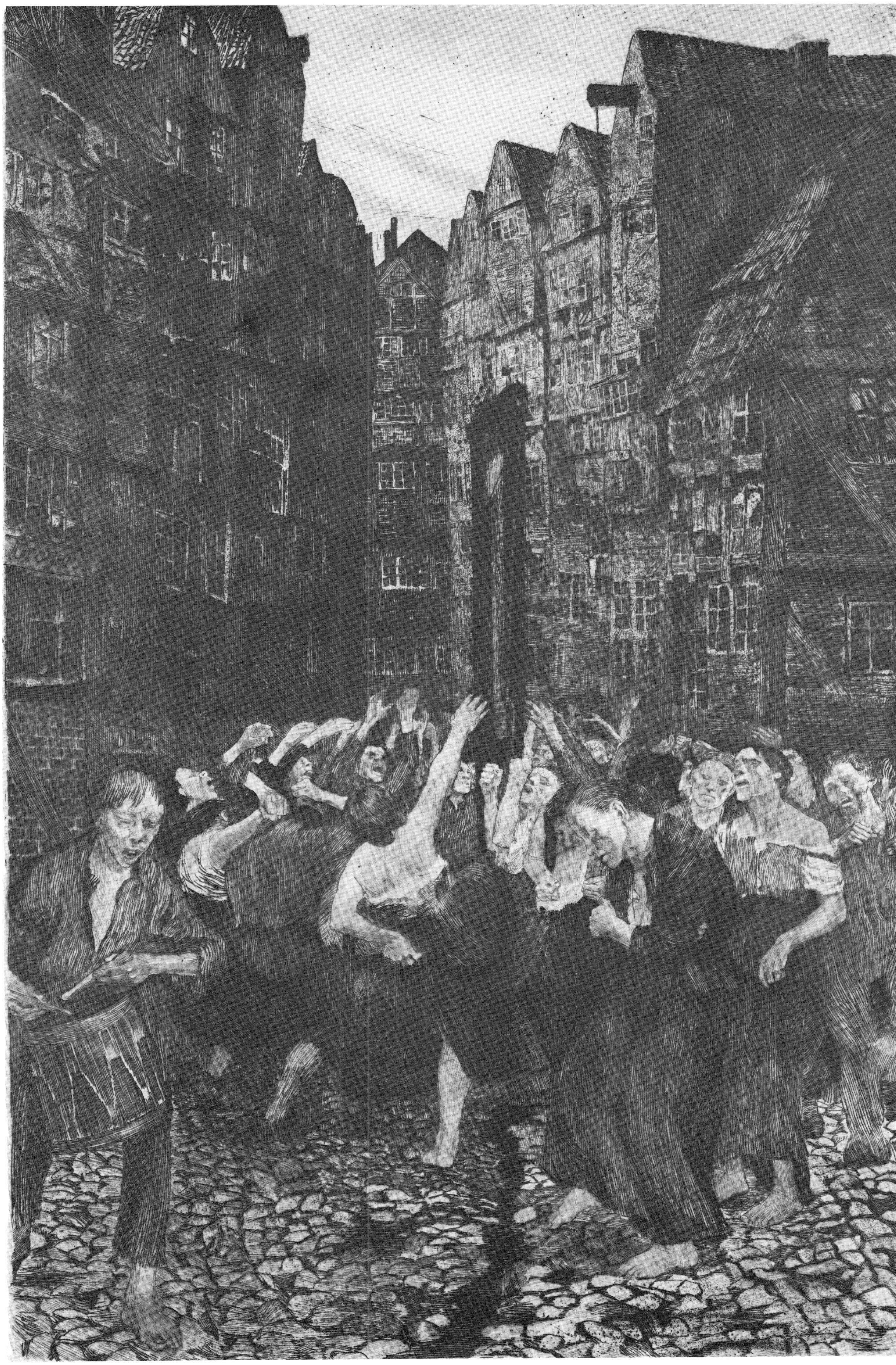

10. La Carmagnole

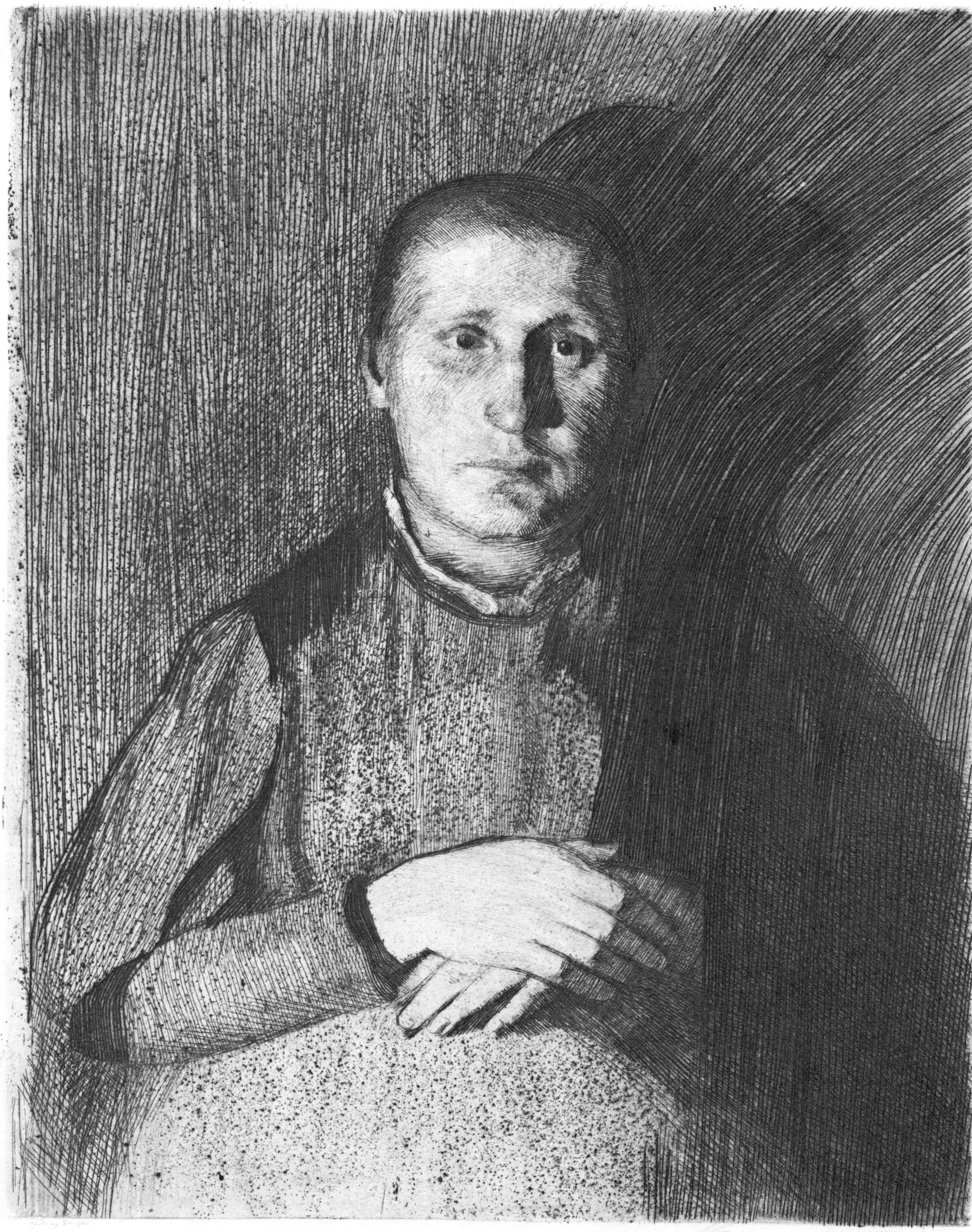

11. Woman with Folded Hands

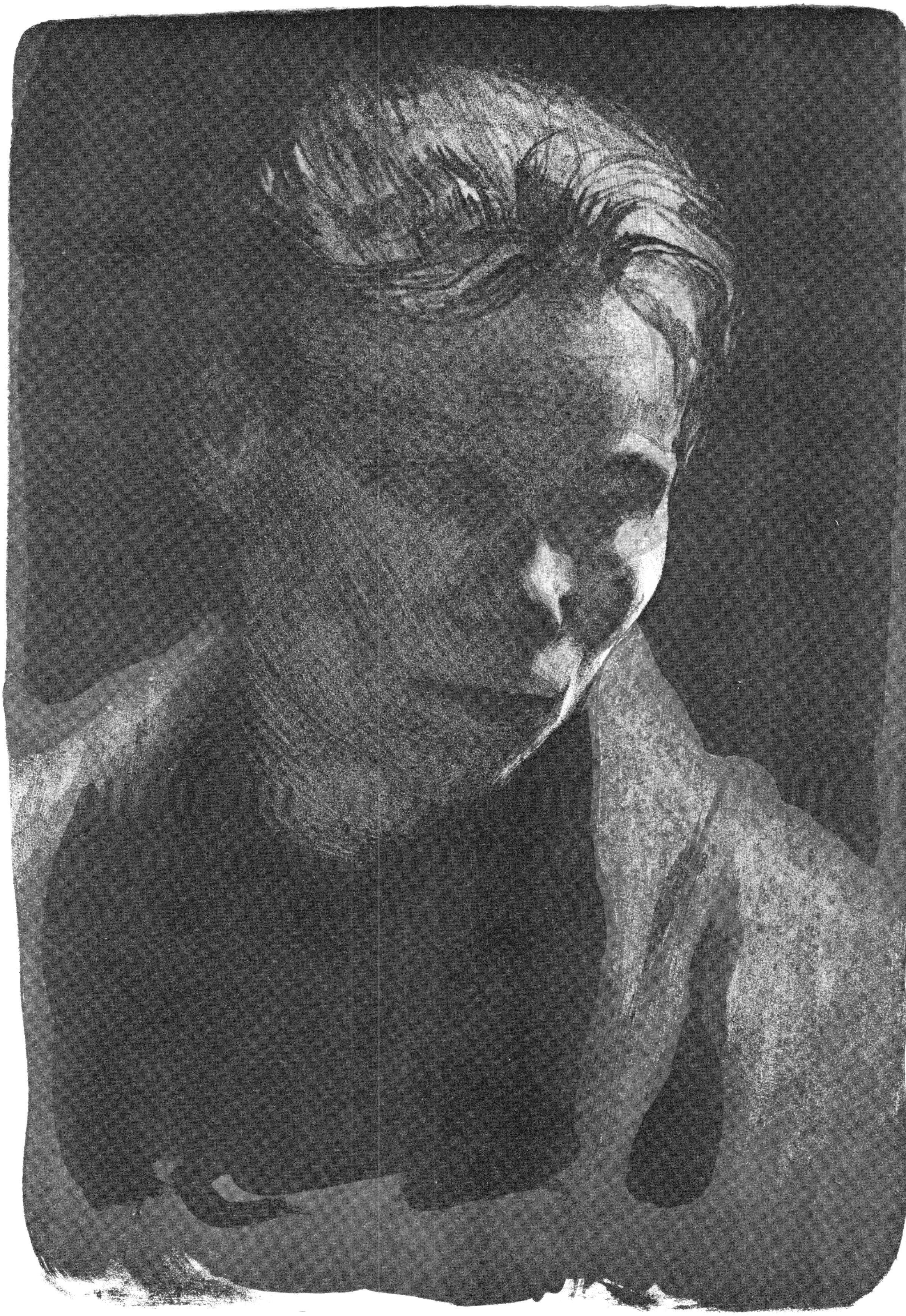

12. Woman with Blue Shawl

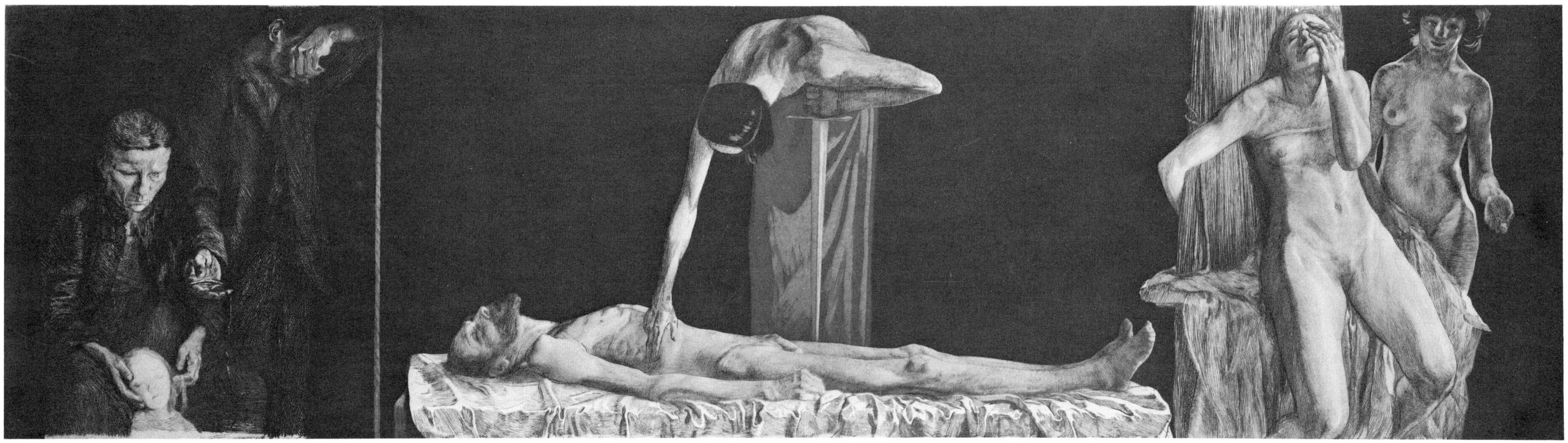

13. The Downtrodden

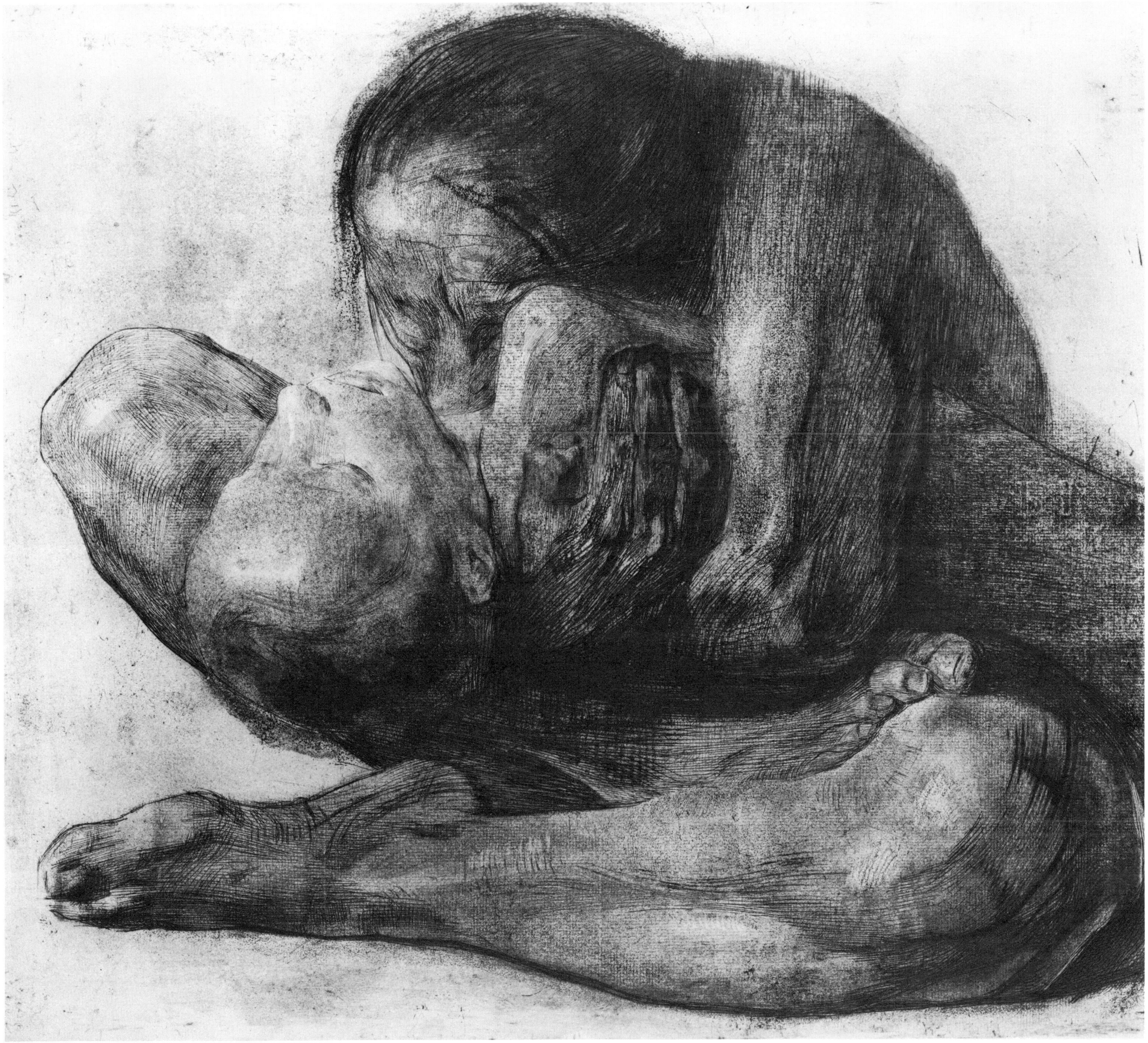

14. Mother with Dead Child

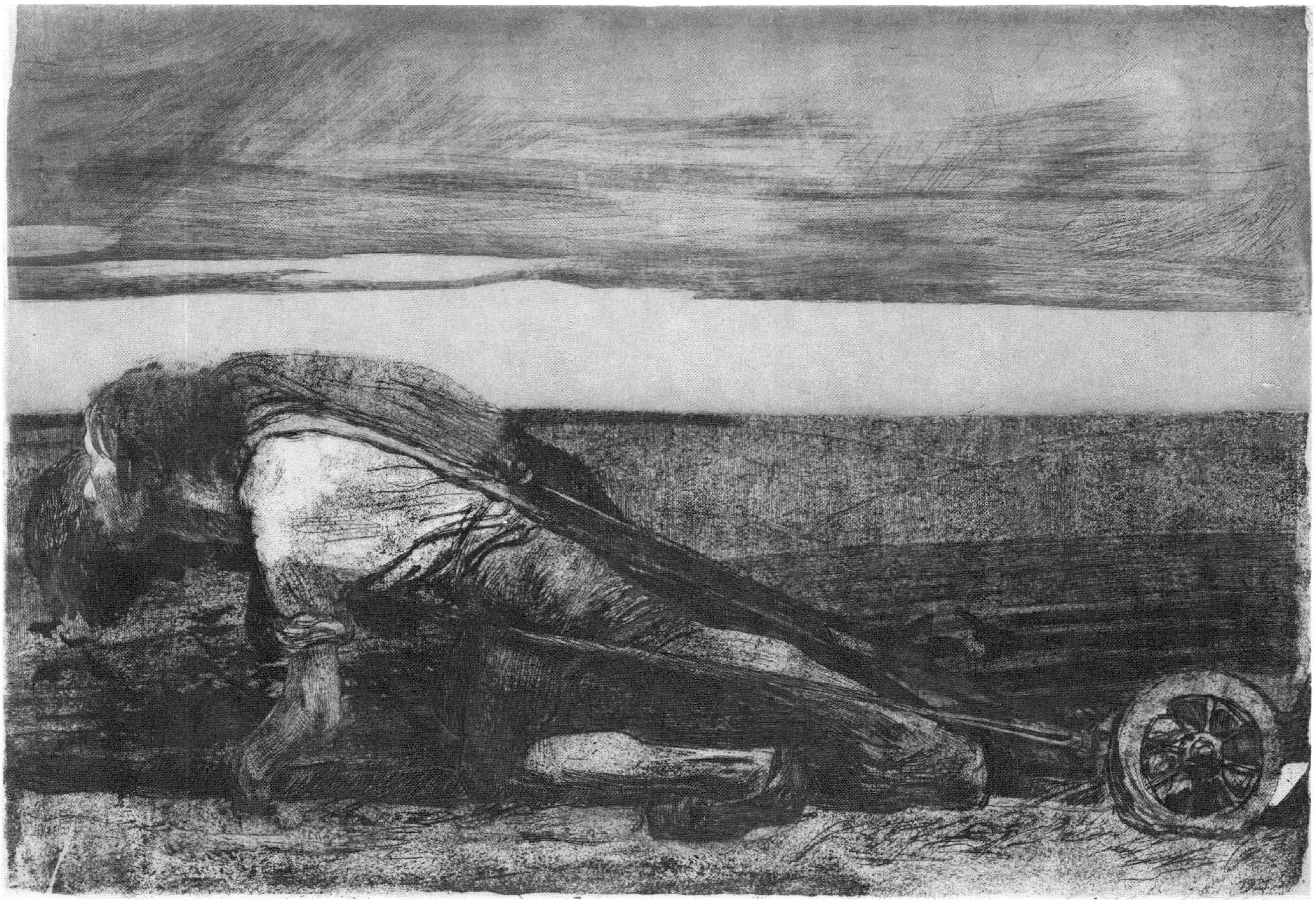

15. Plowing

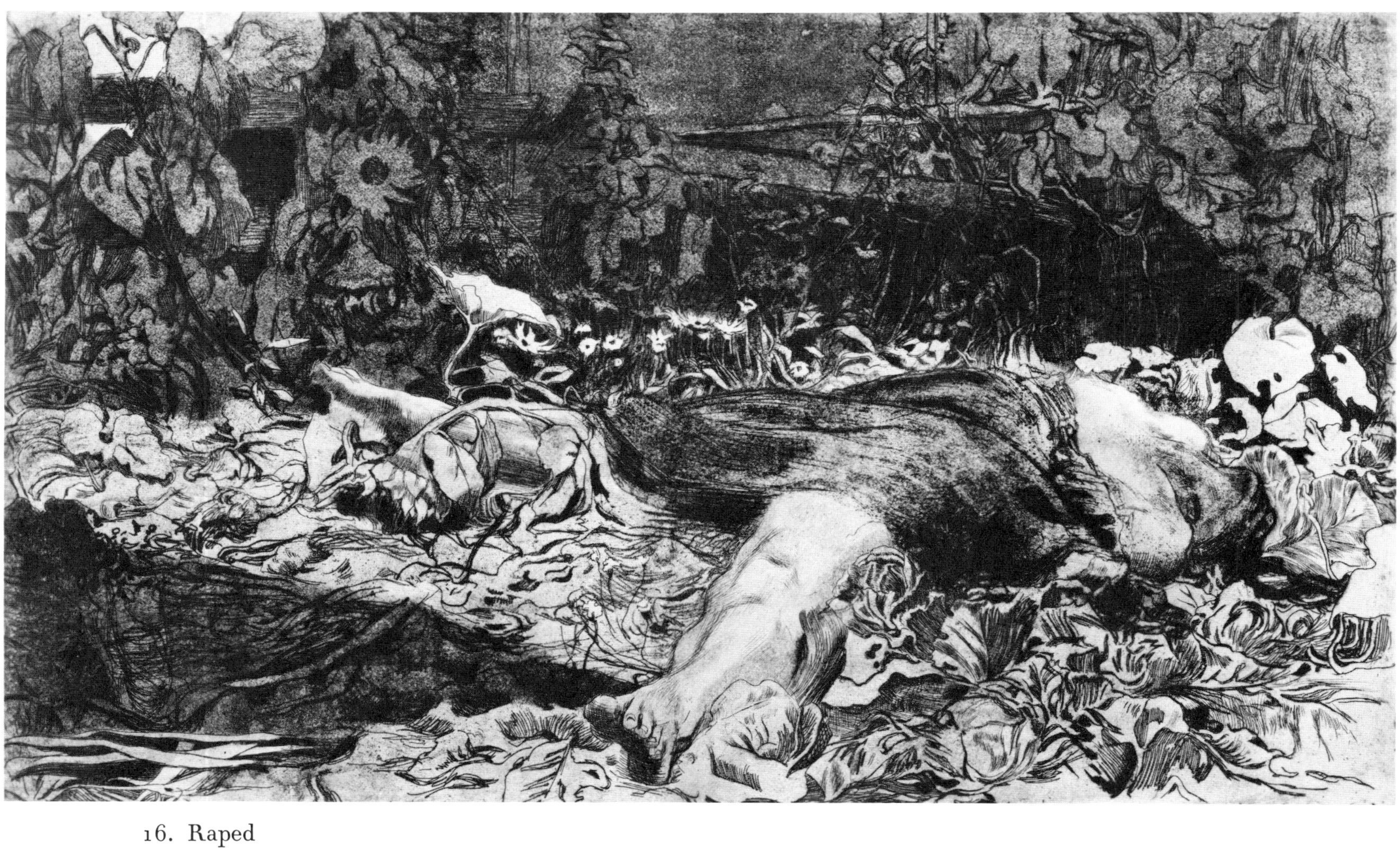

16. Raped

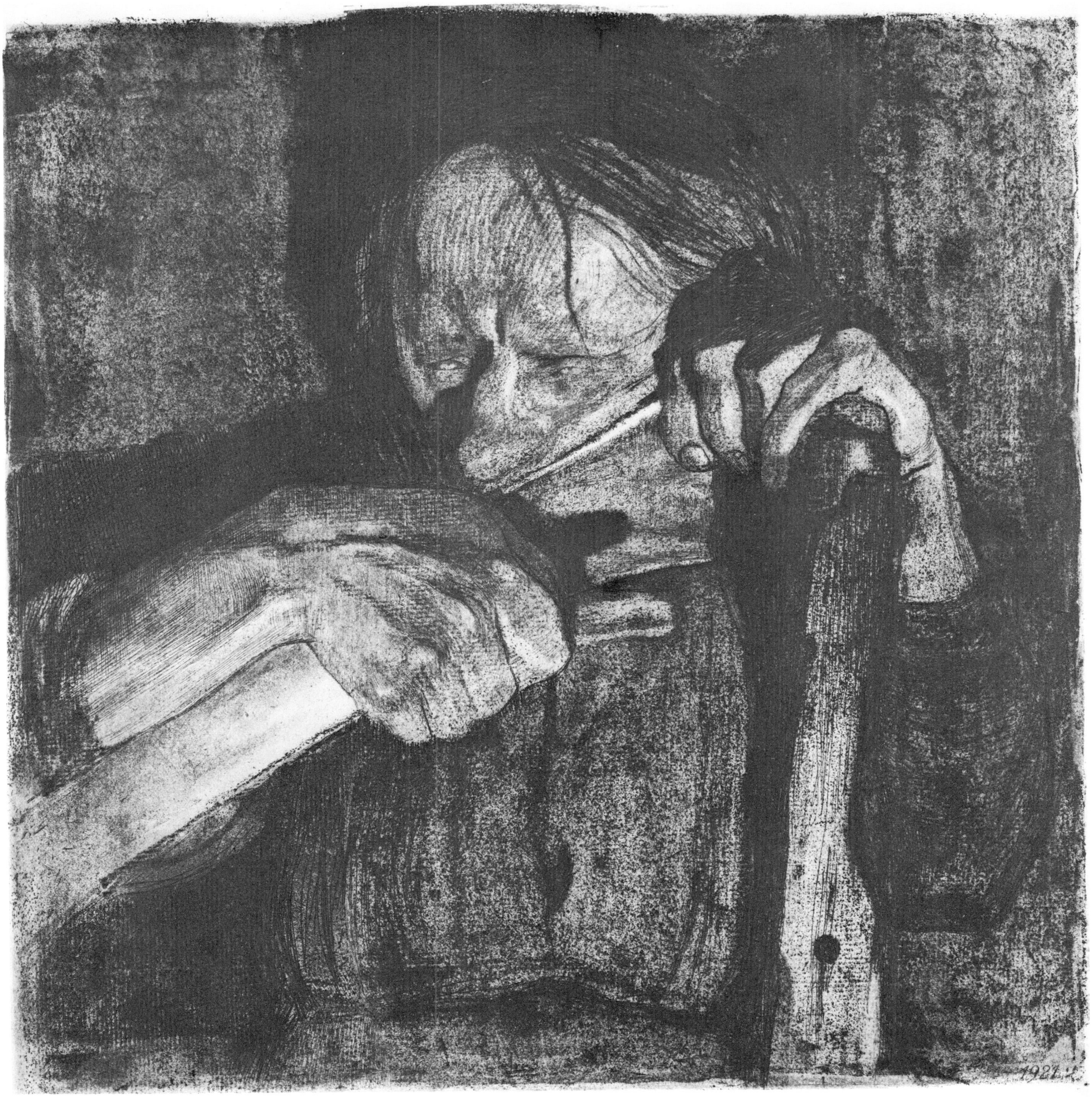

17. Sharpening the Scythe

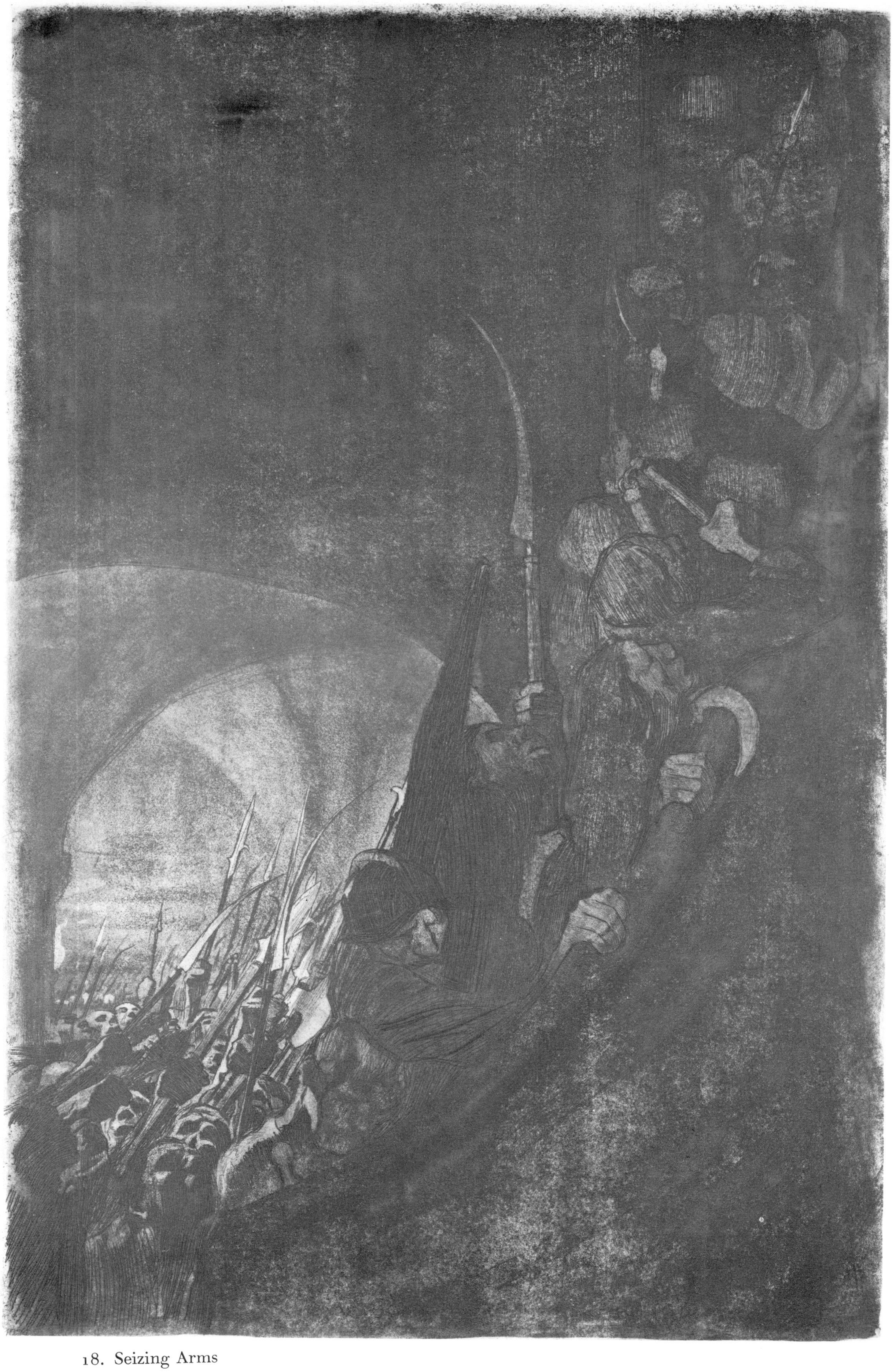

18. Seizing Arms

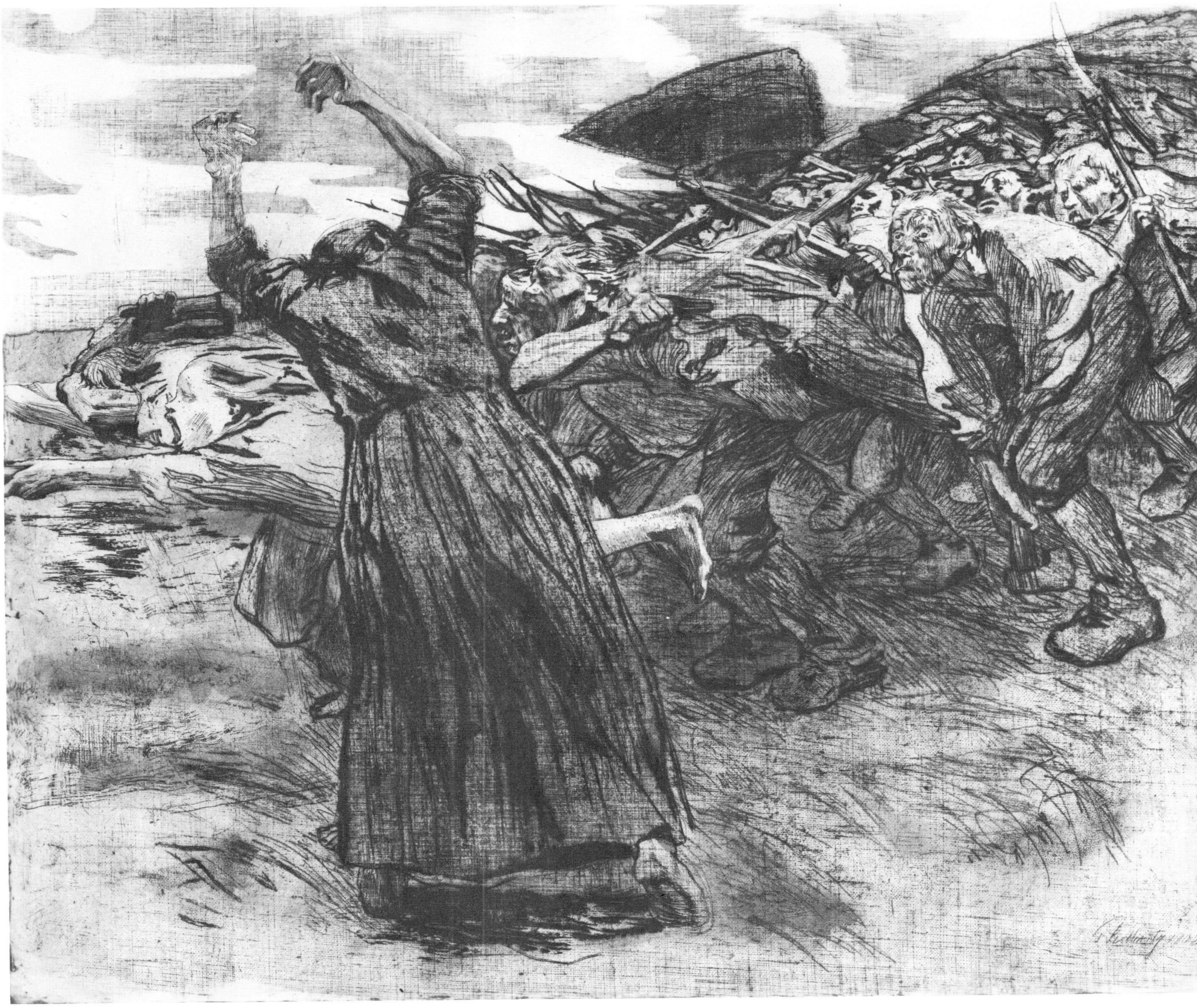

19. Outbreak

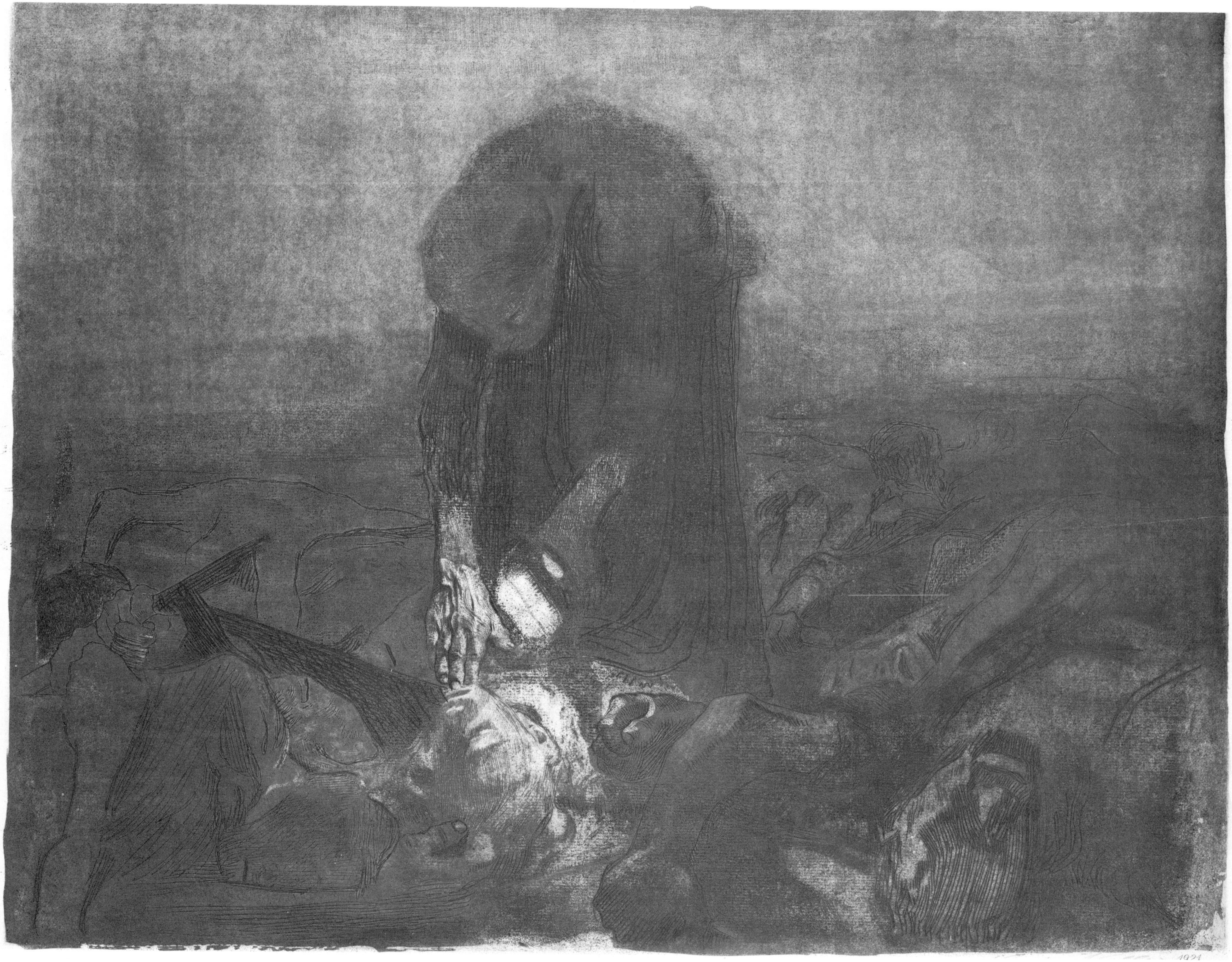

20. After the Battle

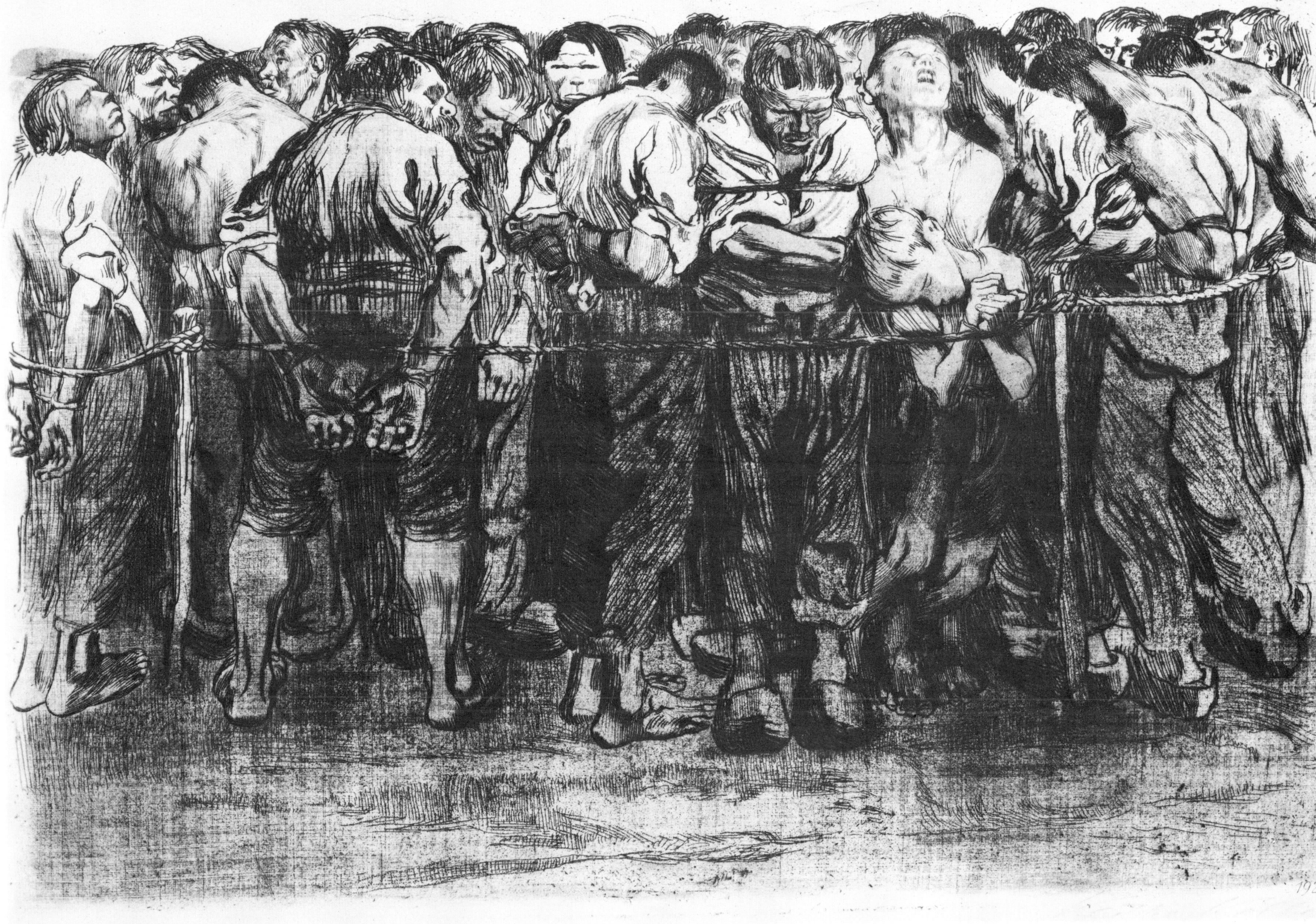

21. The Prisoners

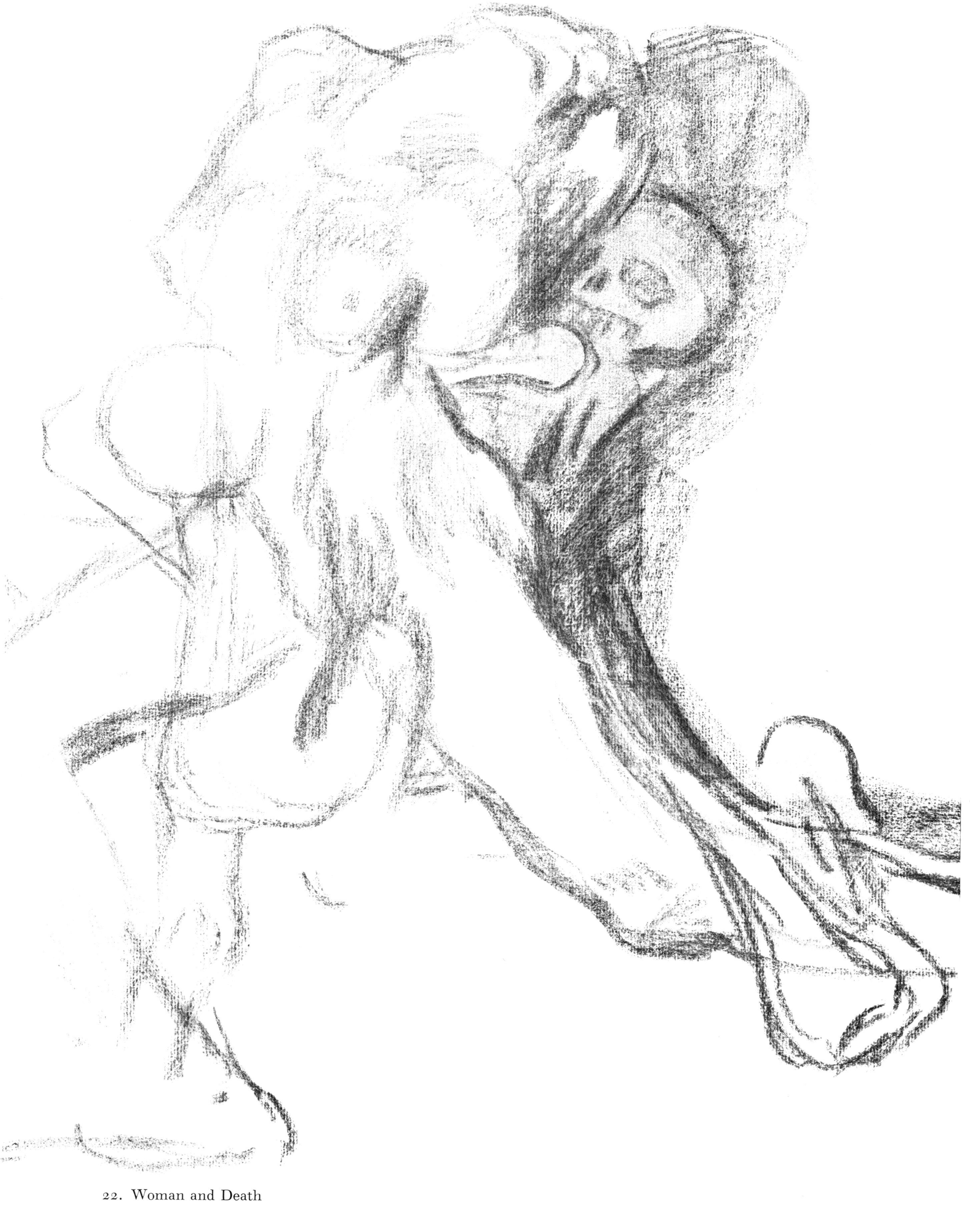

22. Woman and Death

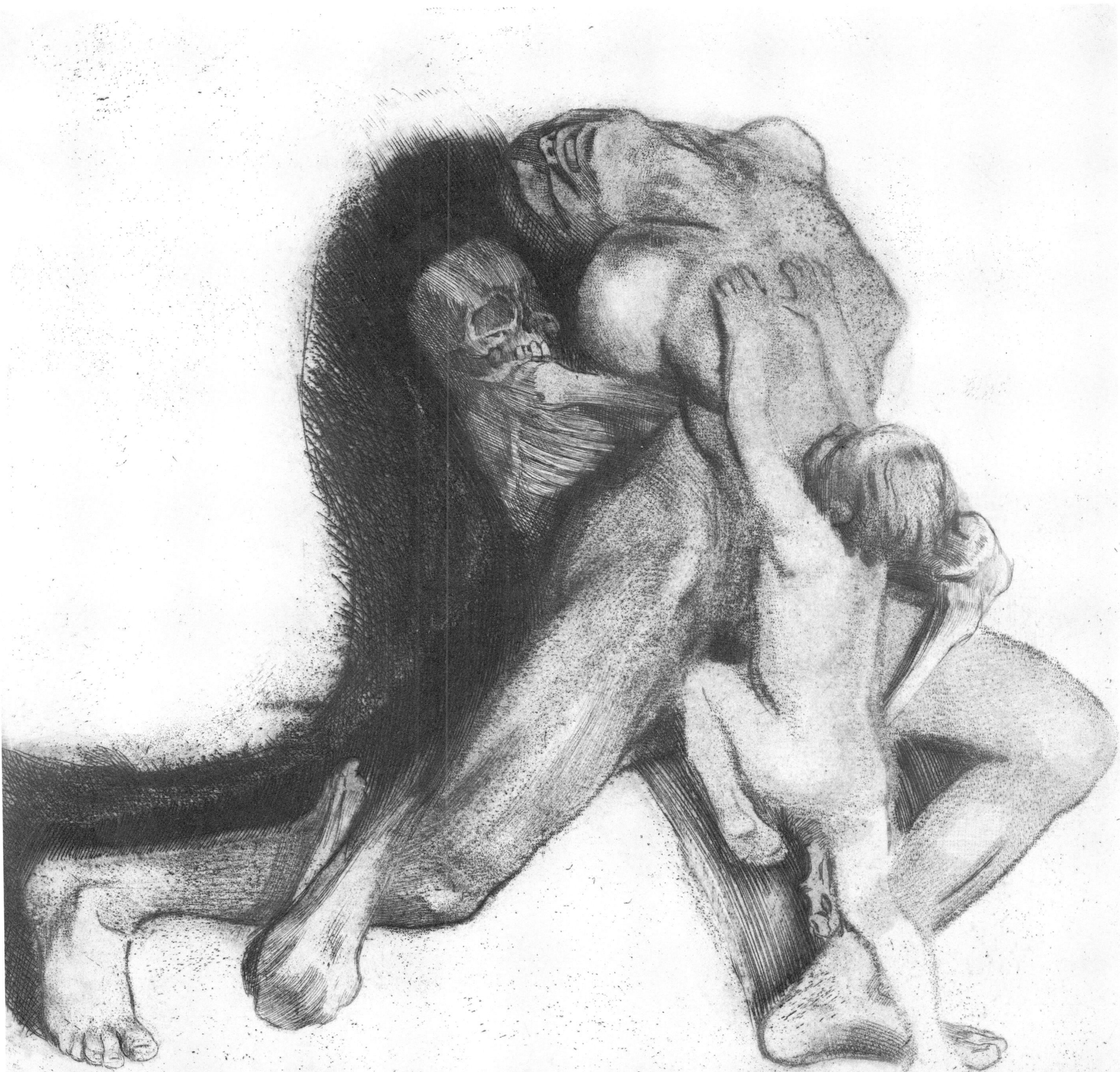

23. Woman and Death

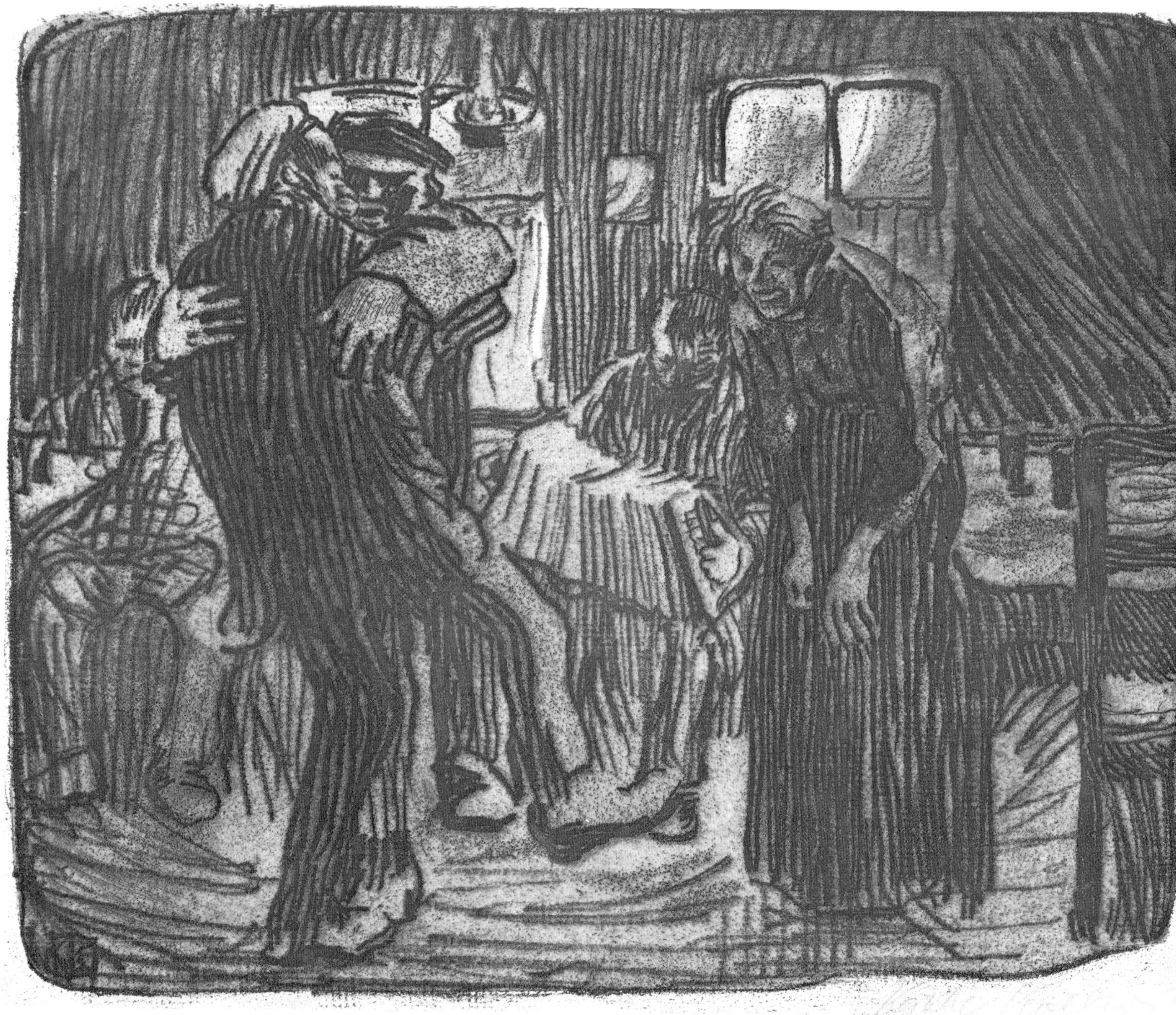

24. Tavern in Hamburg

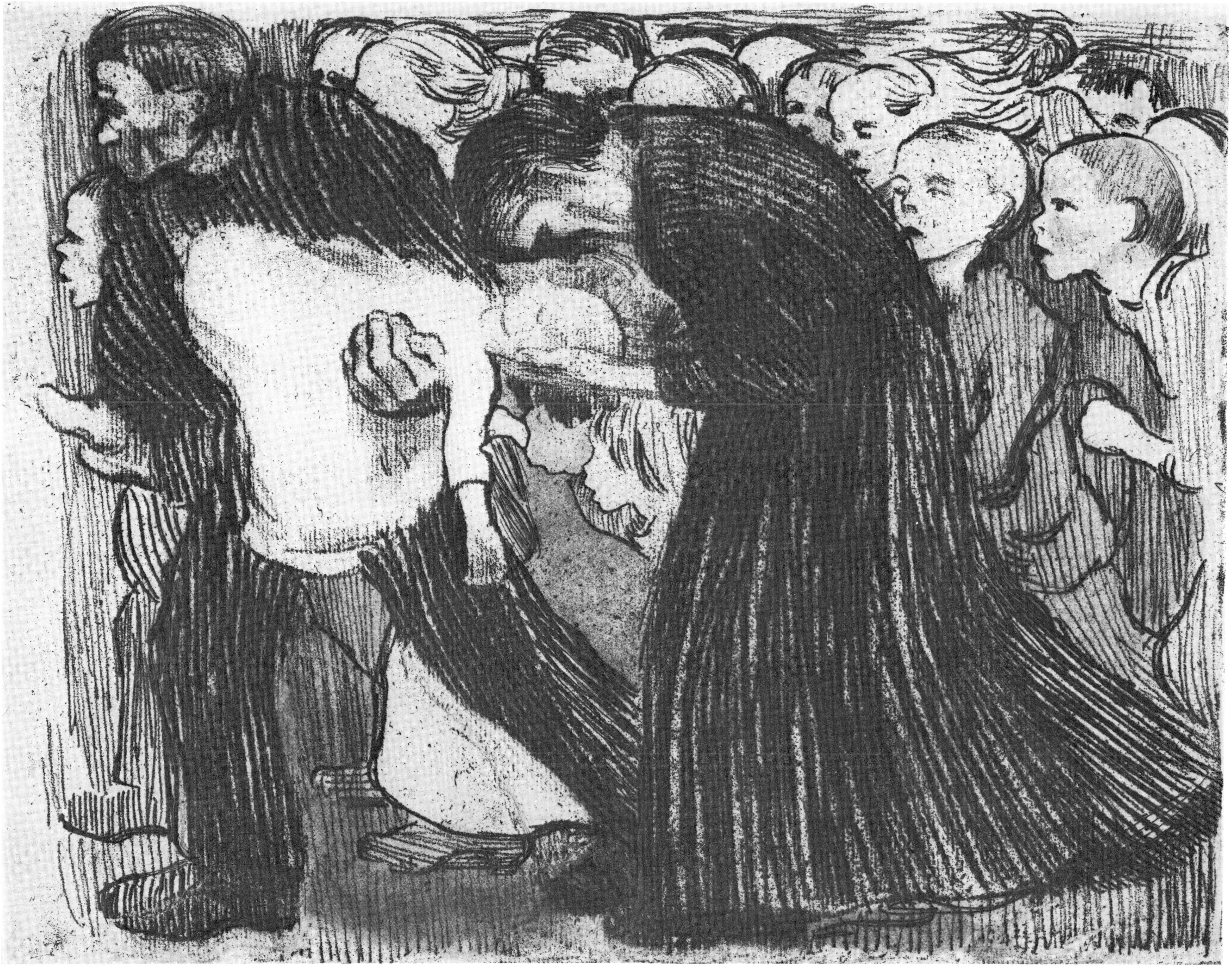

25. Run Over

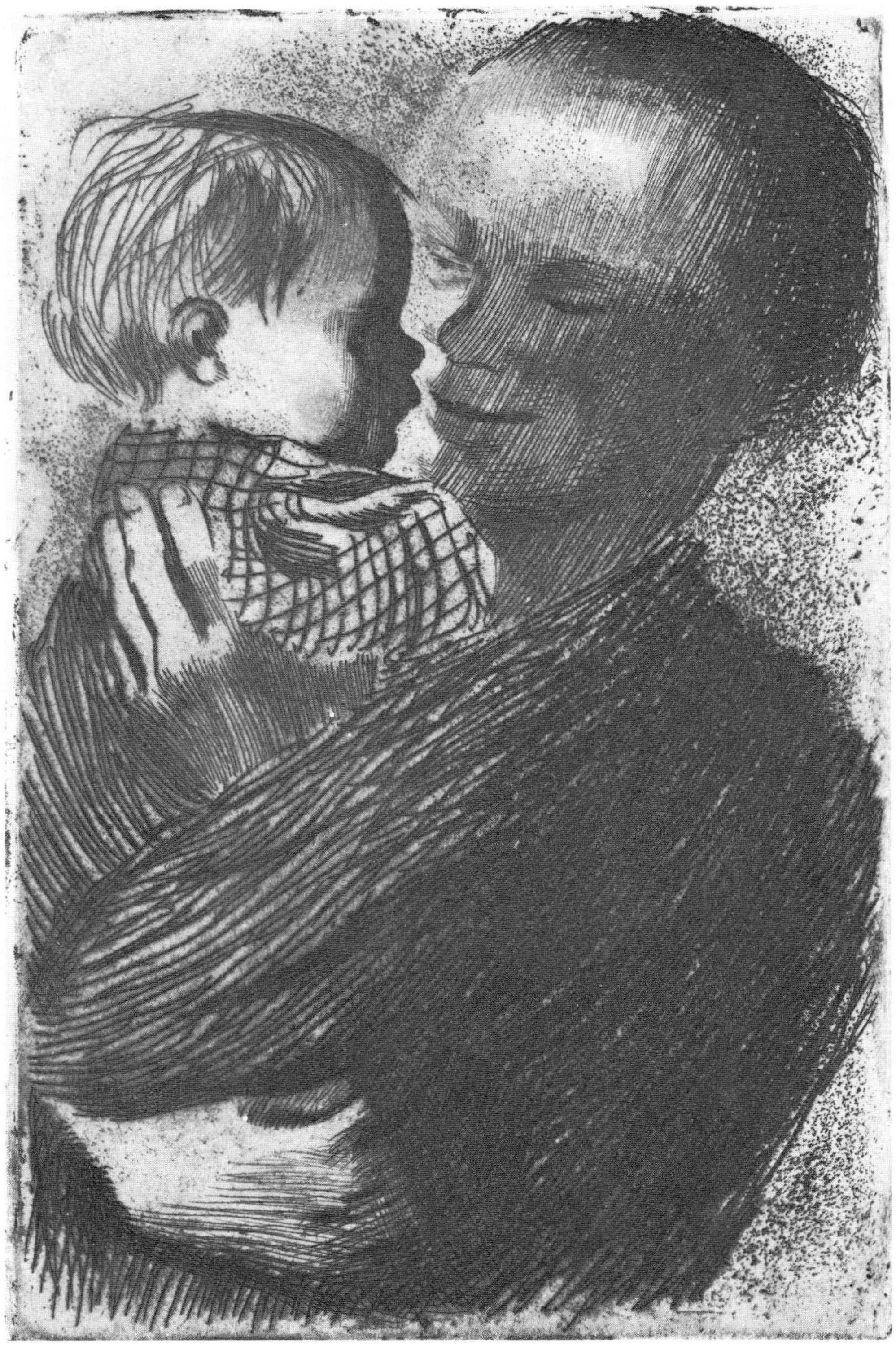

26. Mother with Child in Arms

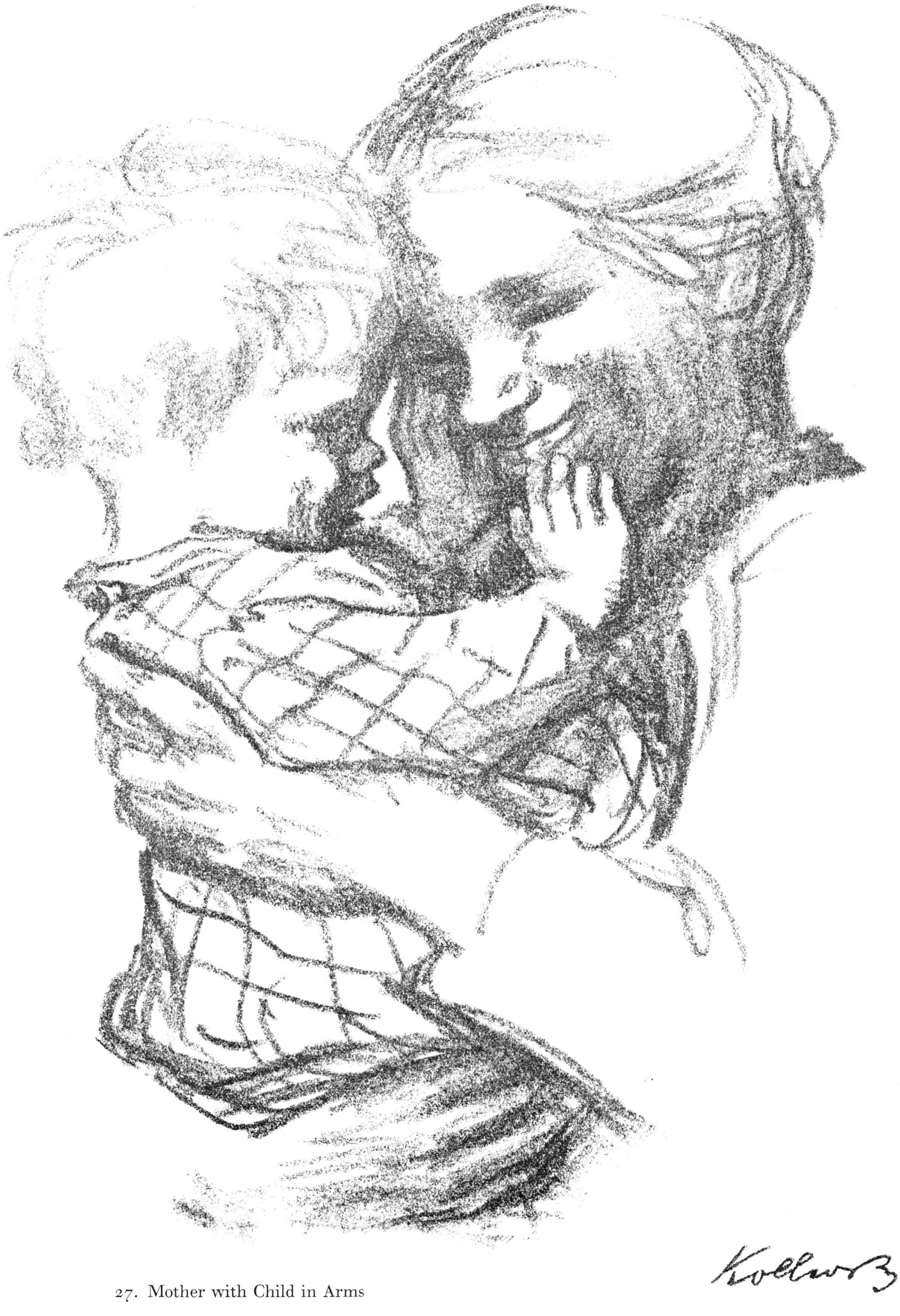

27. Mother with Child in Arms

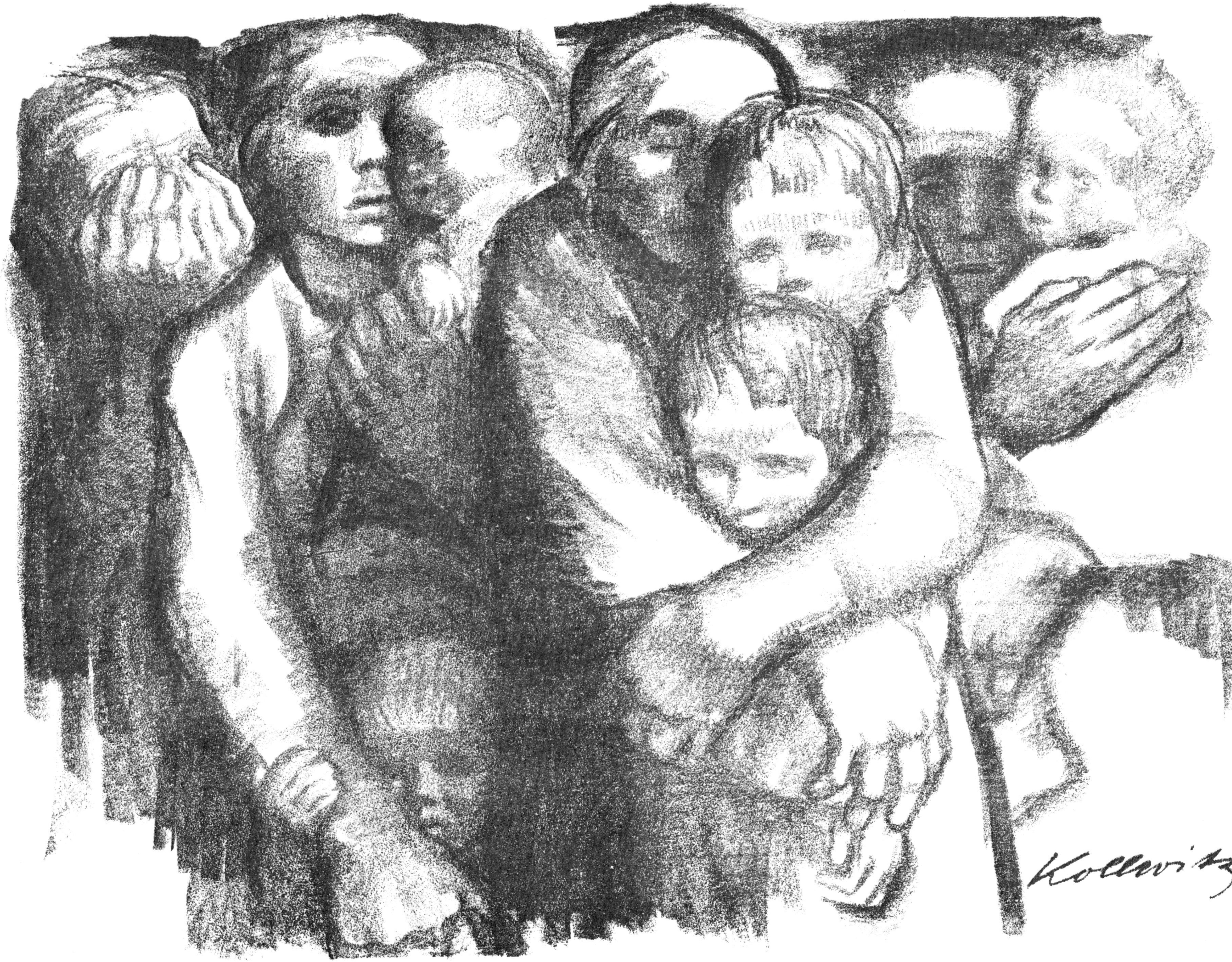

28. The Mothers

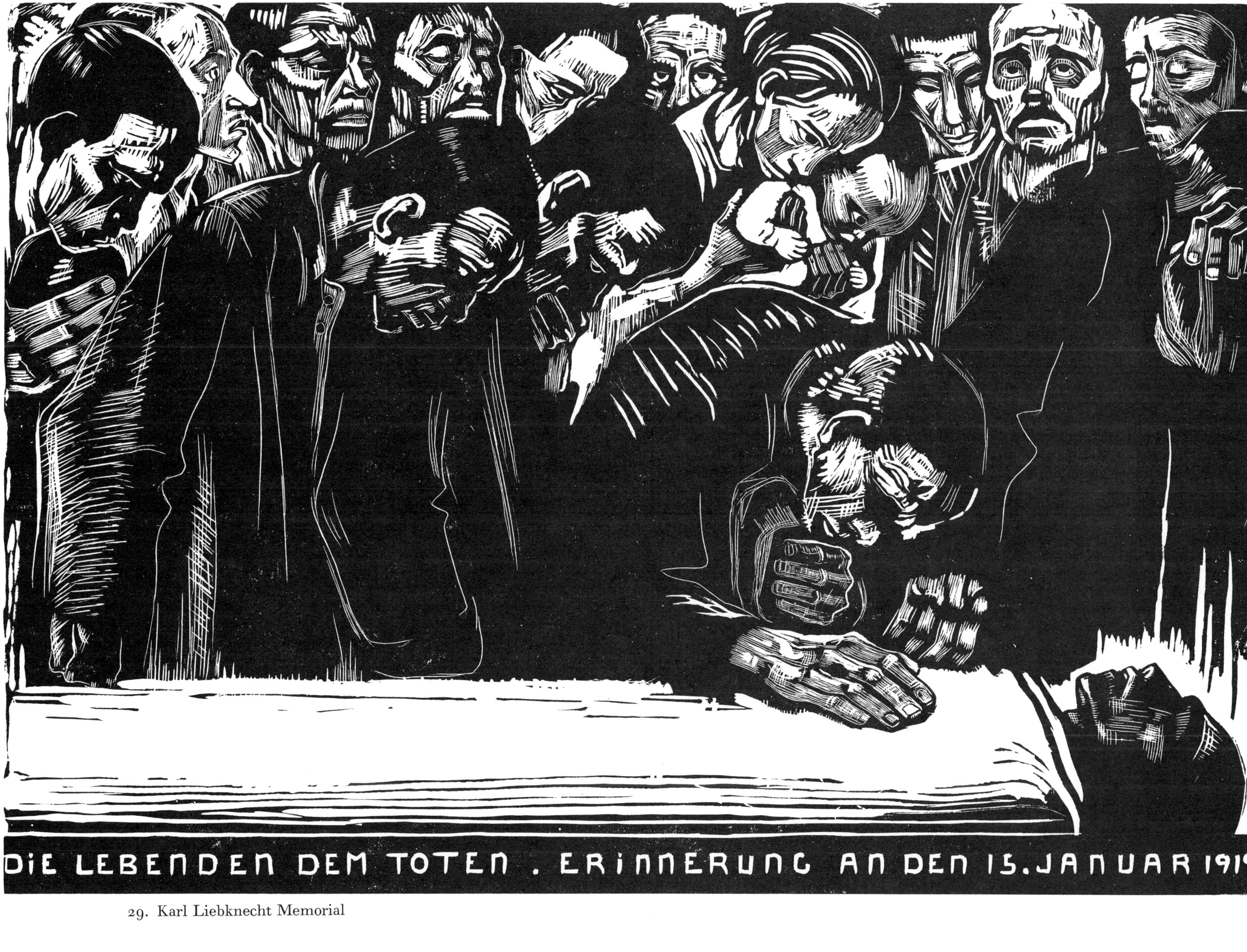

29. Karl Liebknecht Memorial

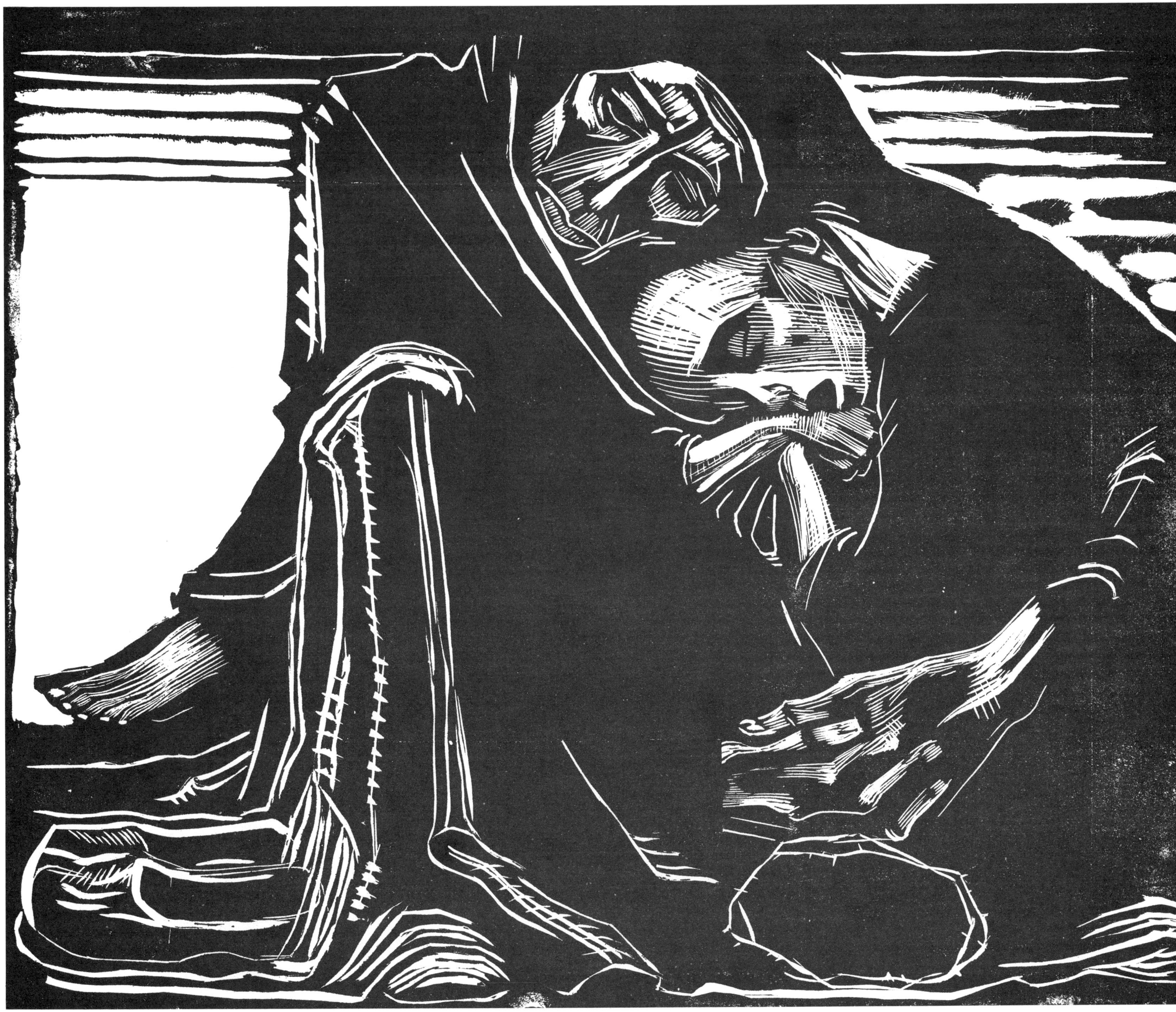

30. Death with Woman in Lap

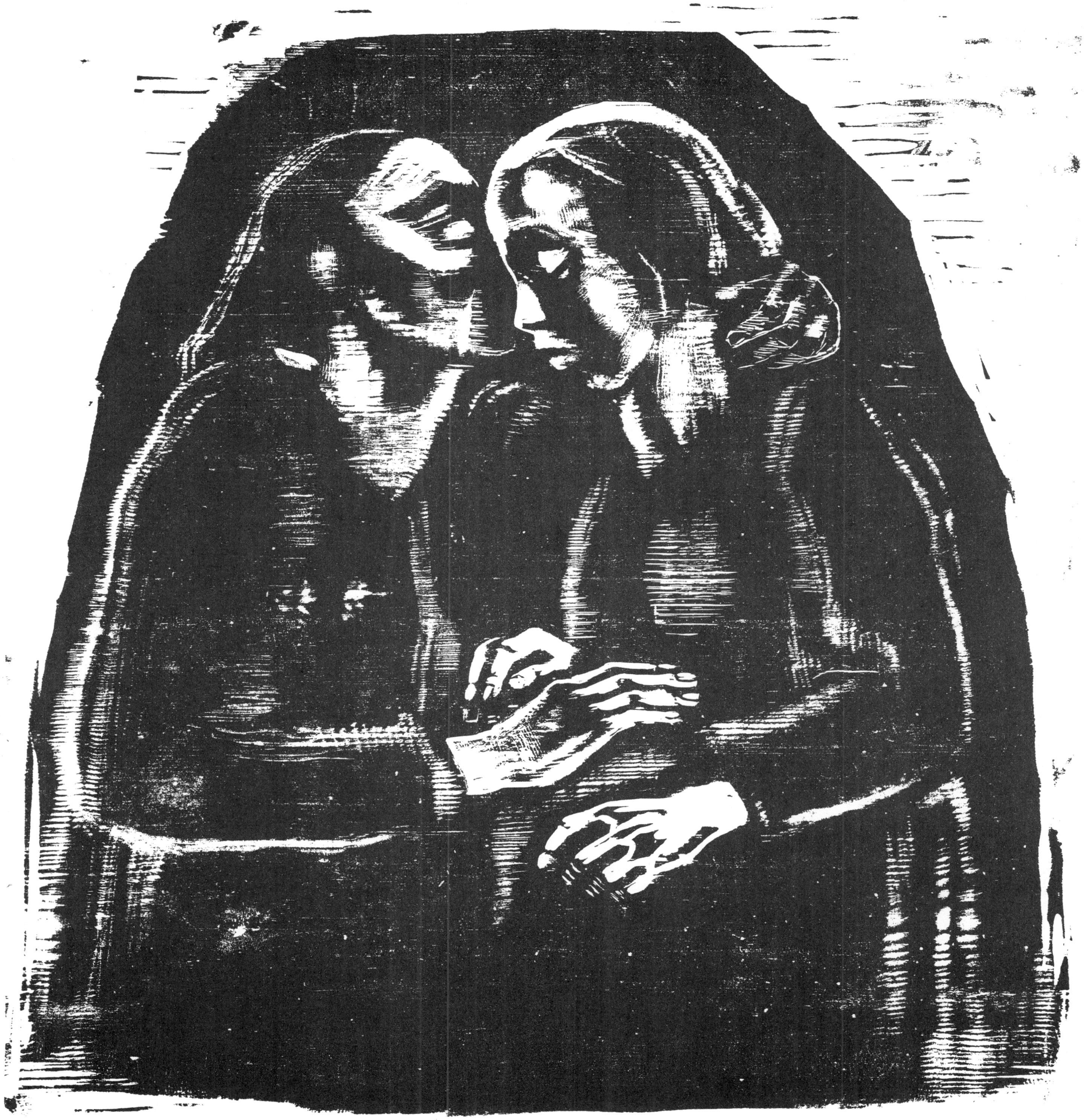

31. Mary and Elizabeth

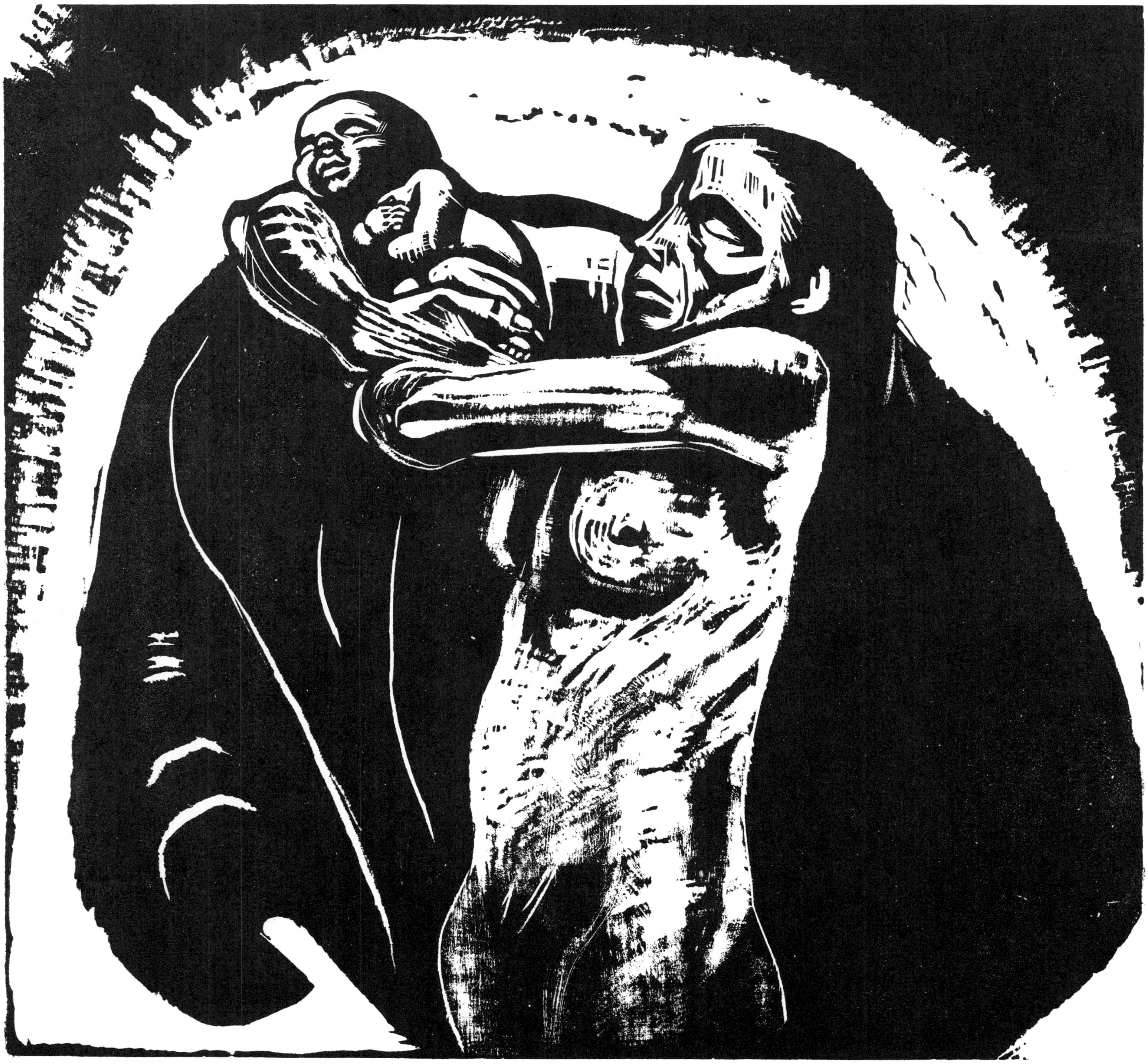

32. The Sacrifice

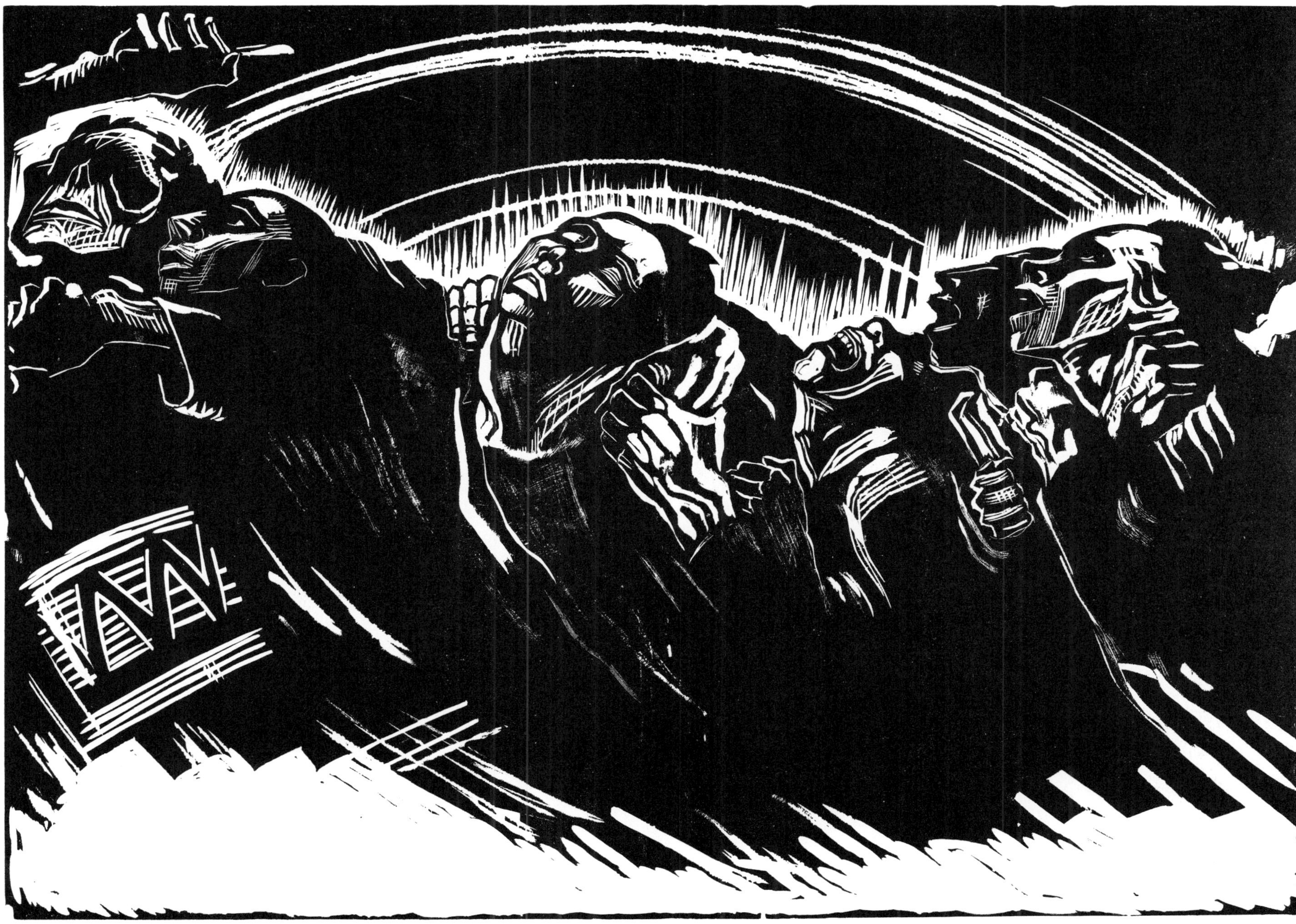

33. The Volunteers

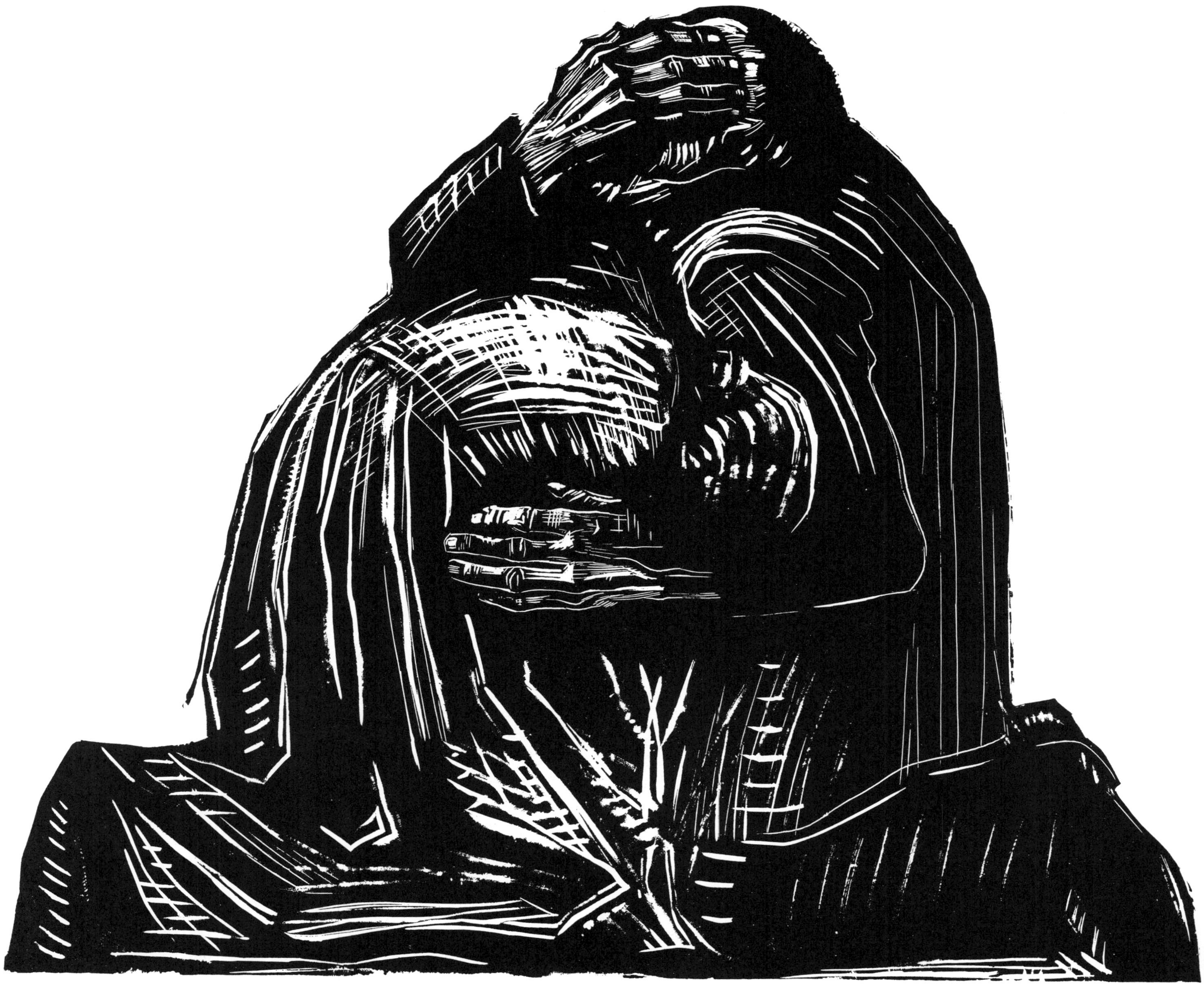

34. The Parents

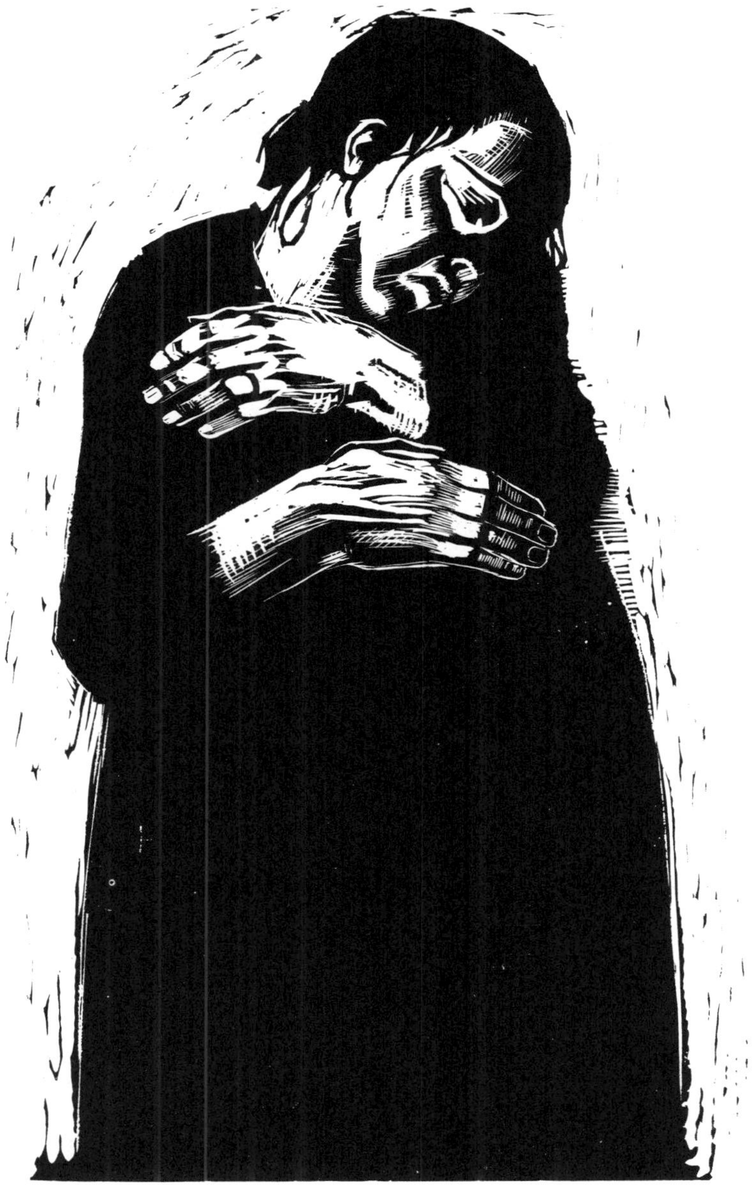

35. The Widow, I

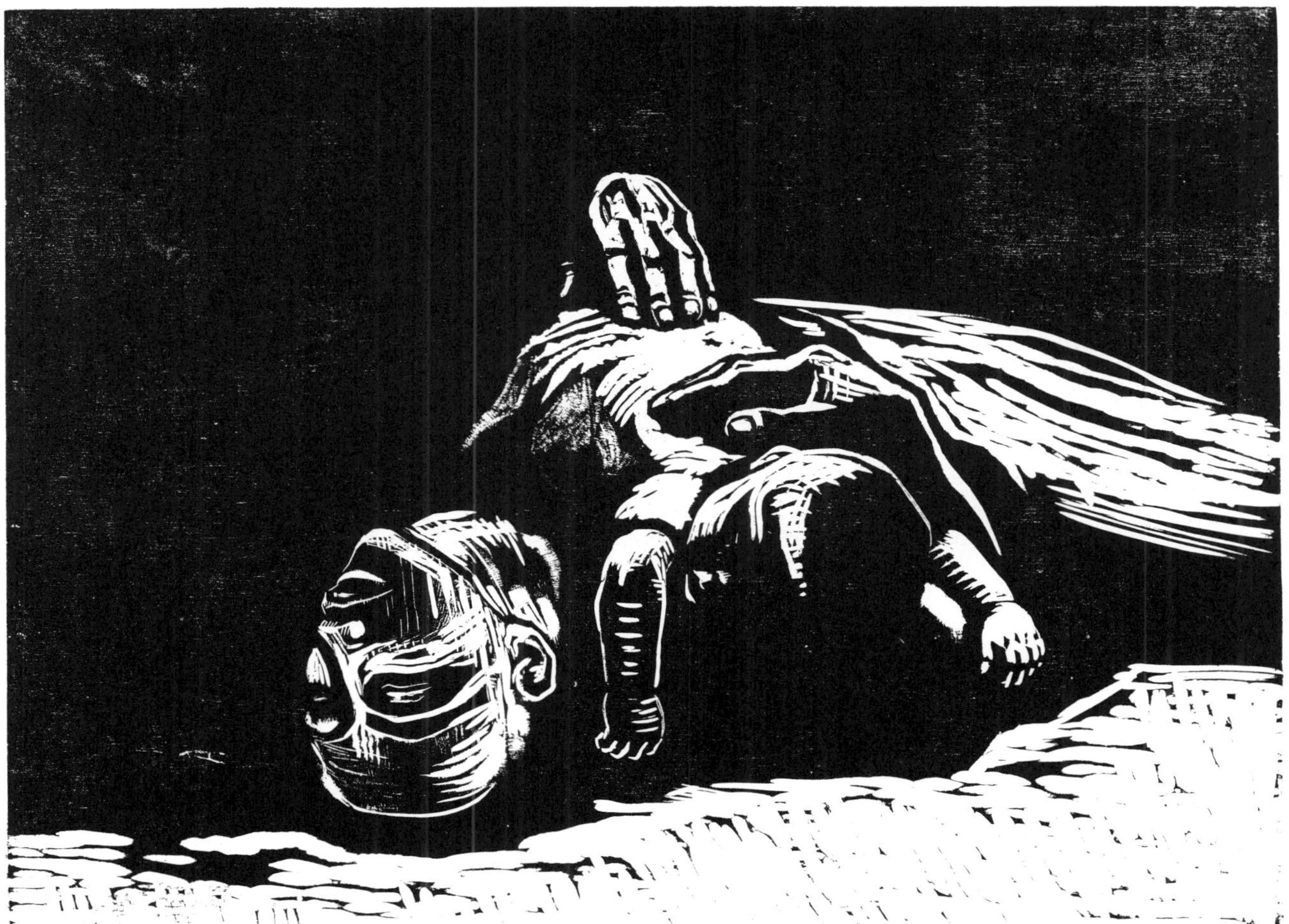

36. The Widow, II

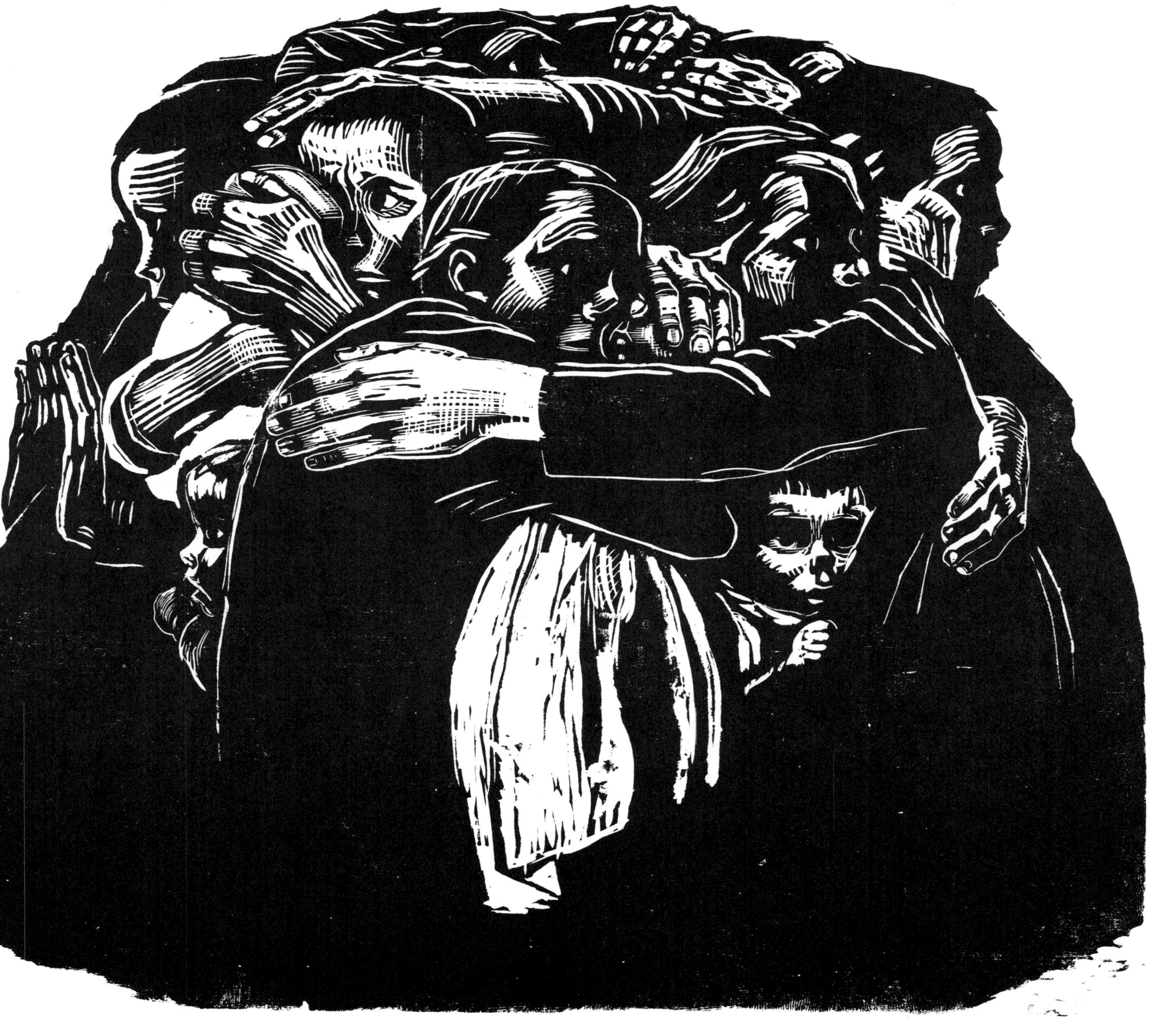

37. The Mothers

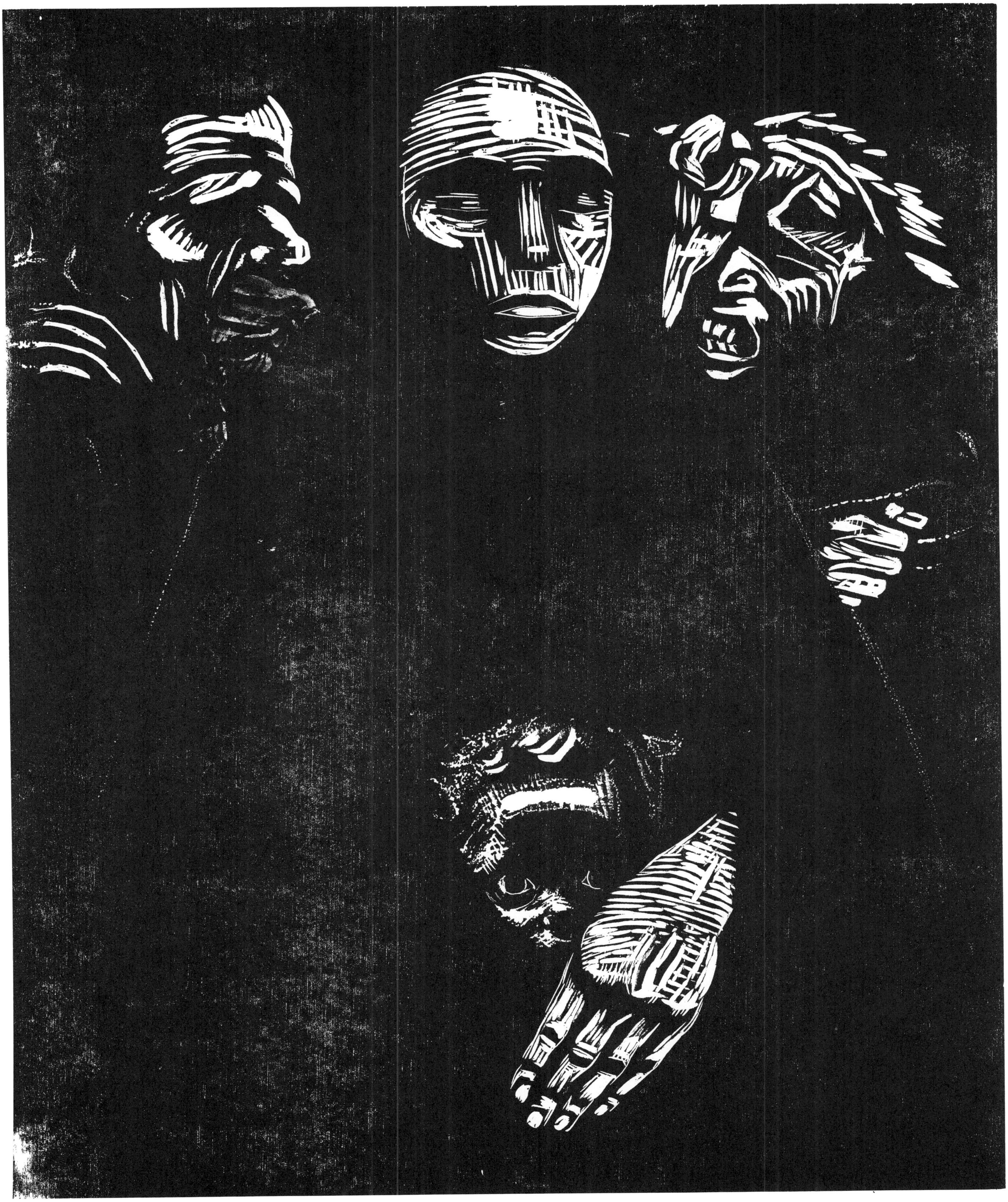

38. The People

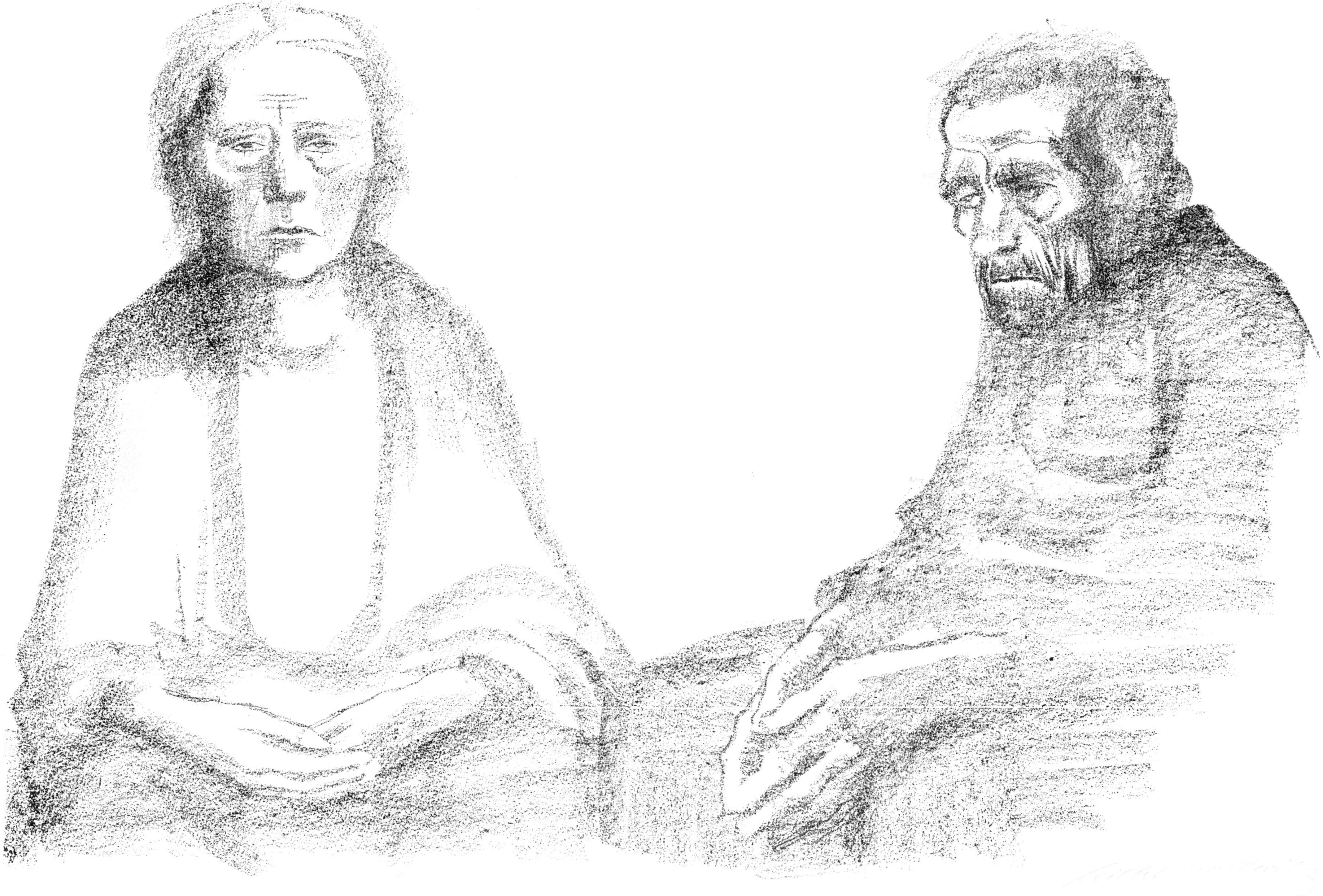

39. The Parents of Käthe Kollwitz

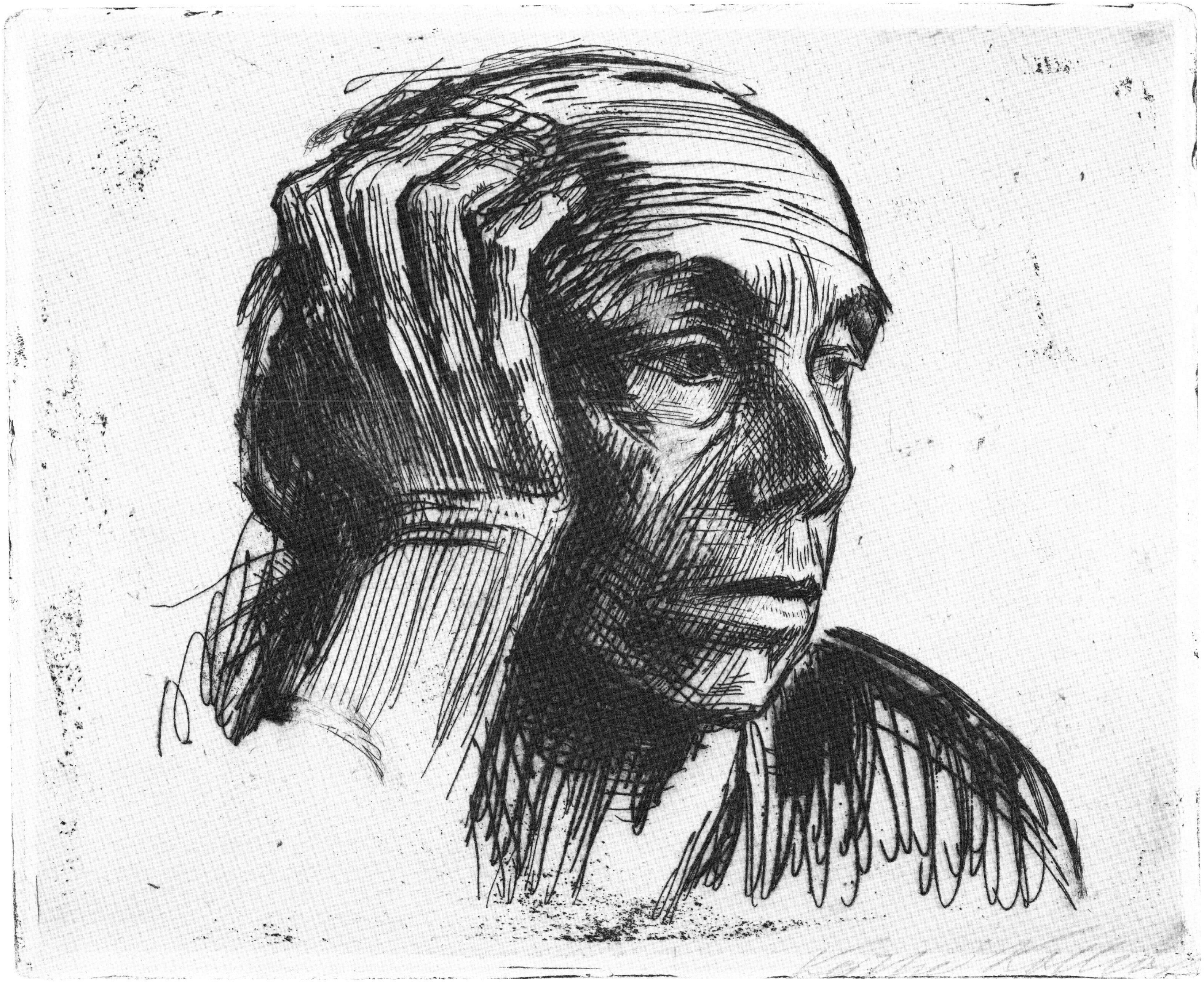

40. Self Portrait, 1921

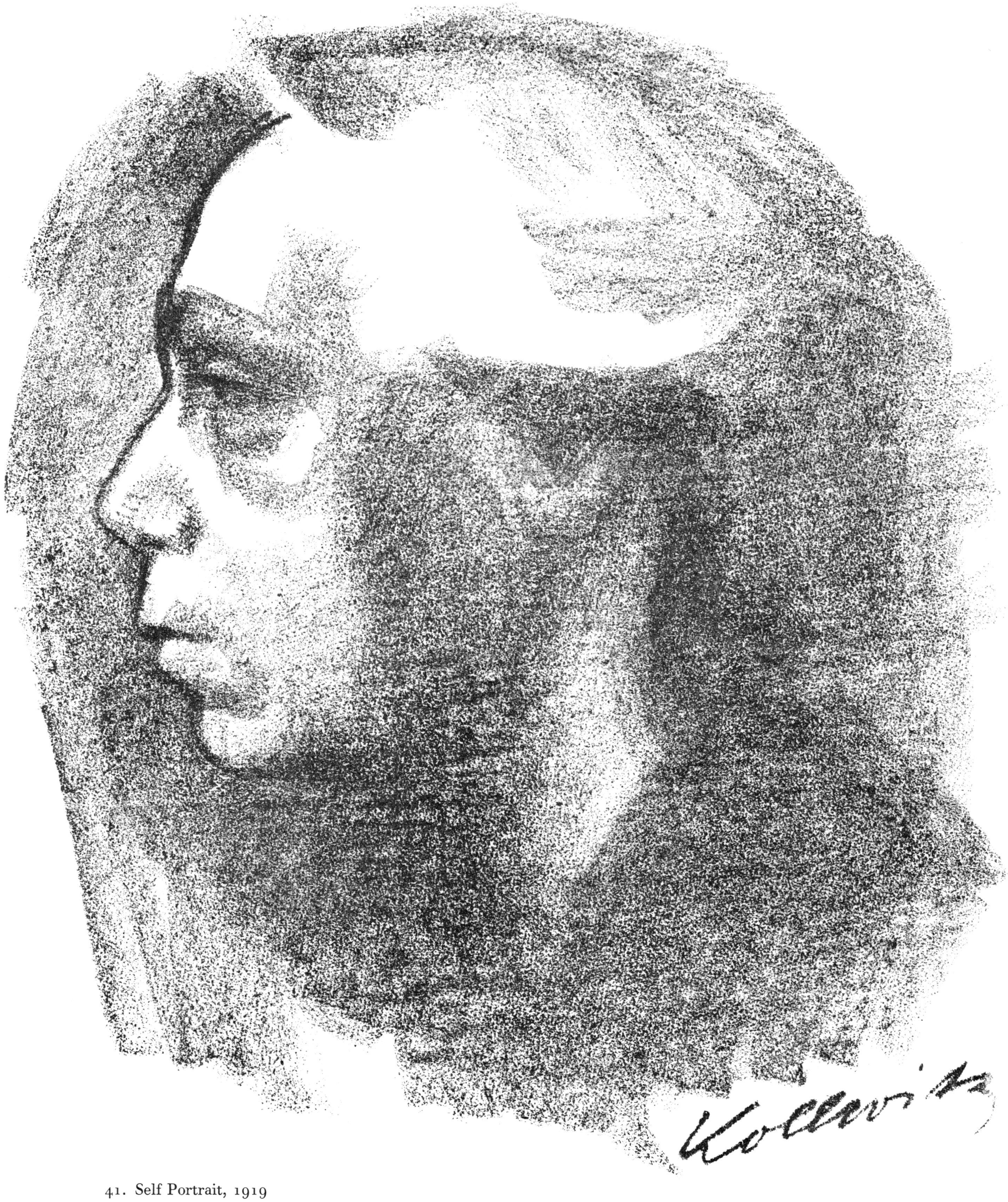

41. Self Portrait, 1919

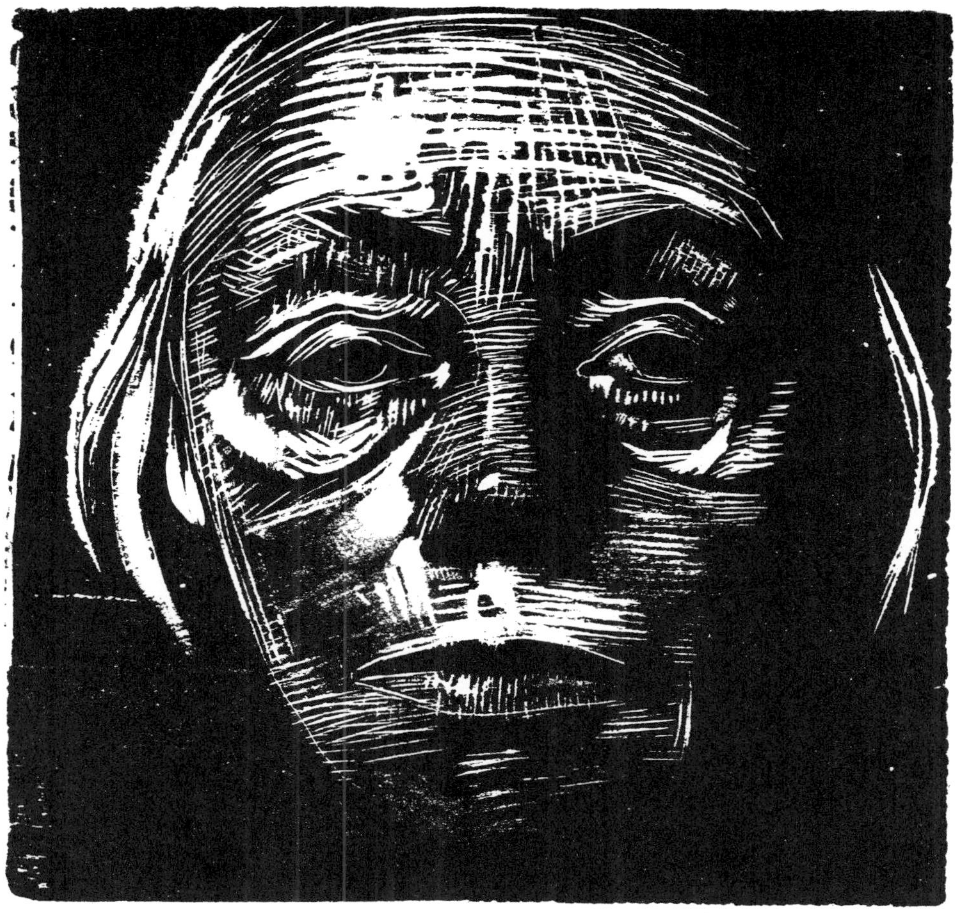

42. Self Portrait, 1923

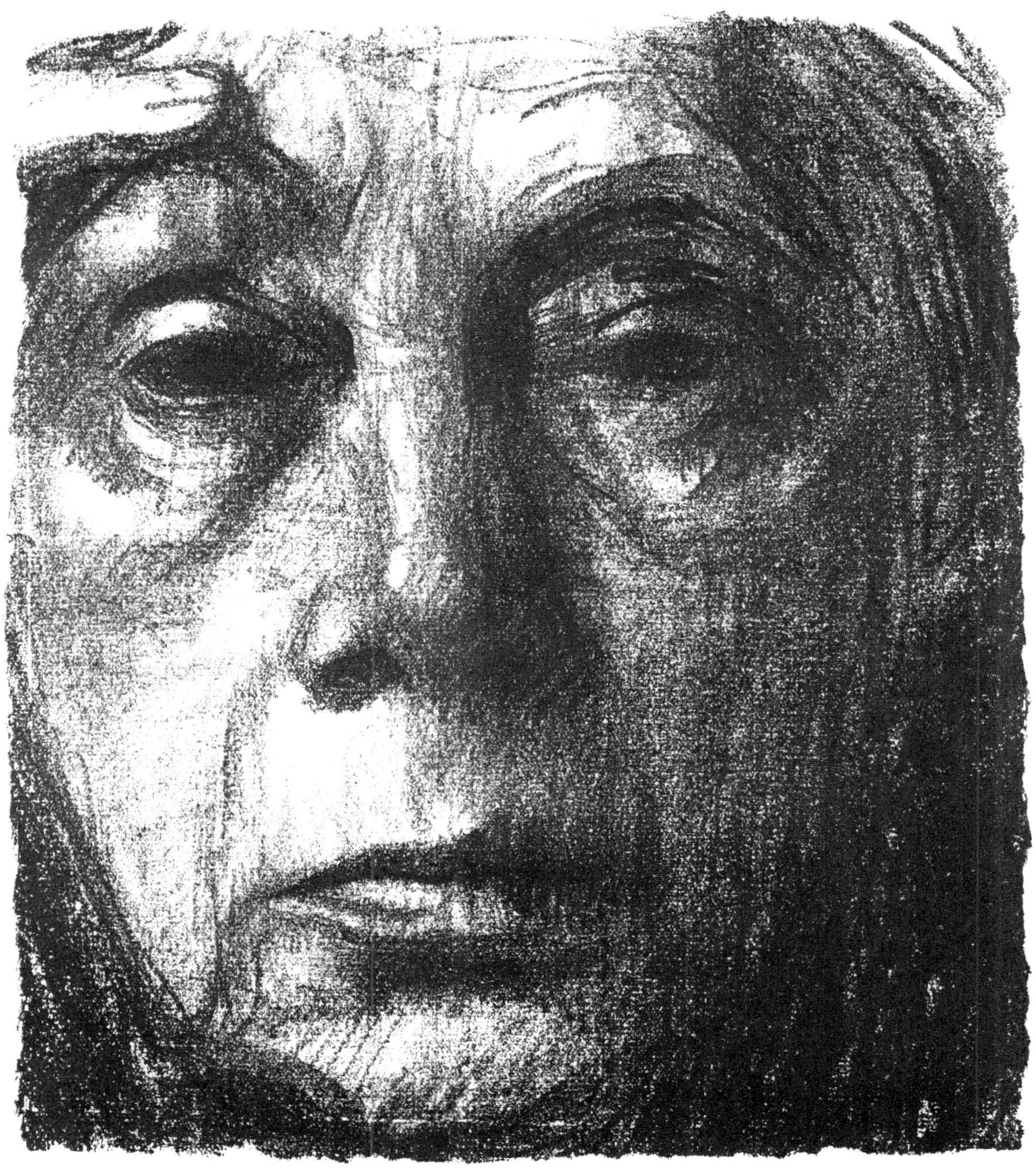

43. Self Portrait, 1934

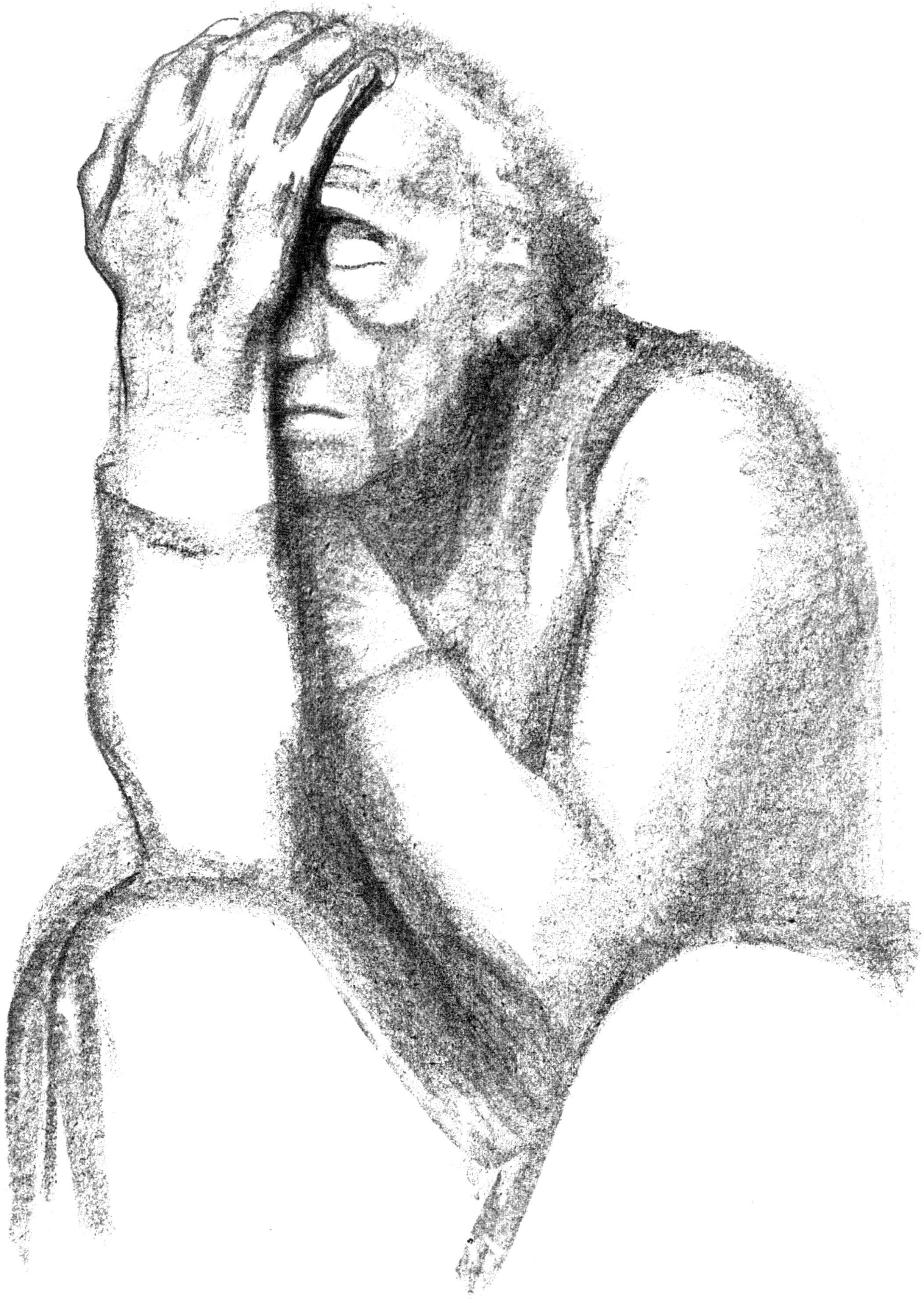

44. Woman Reflecting

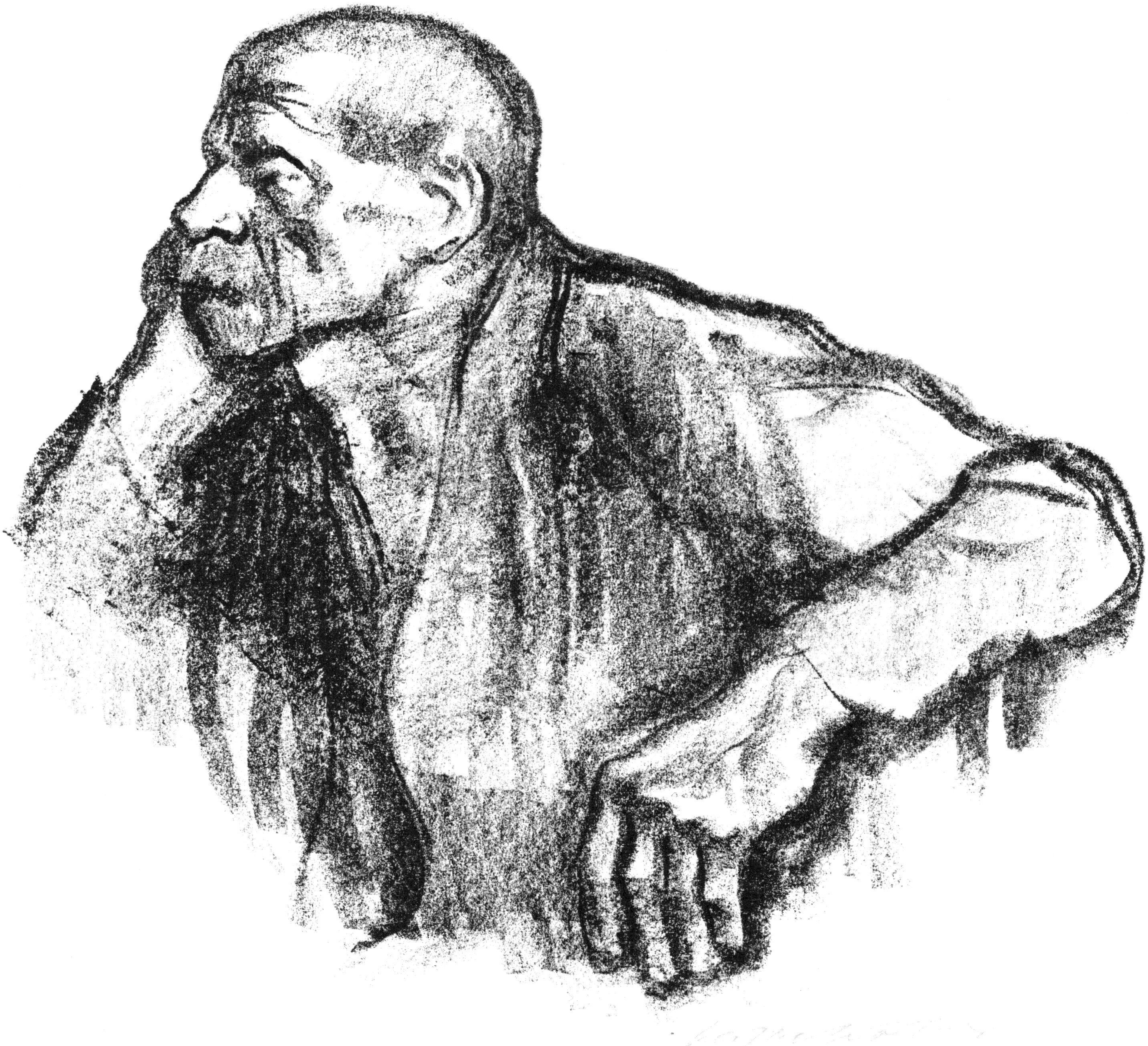

45. Laborer Seated

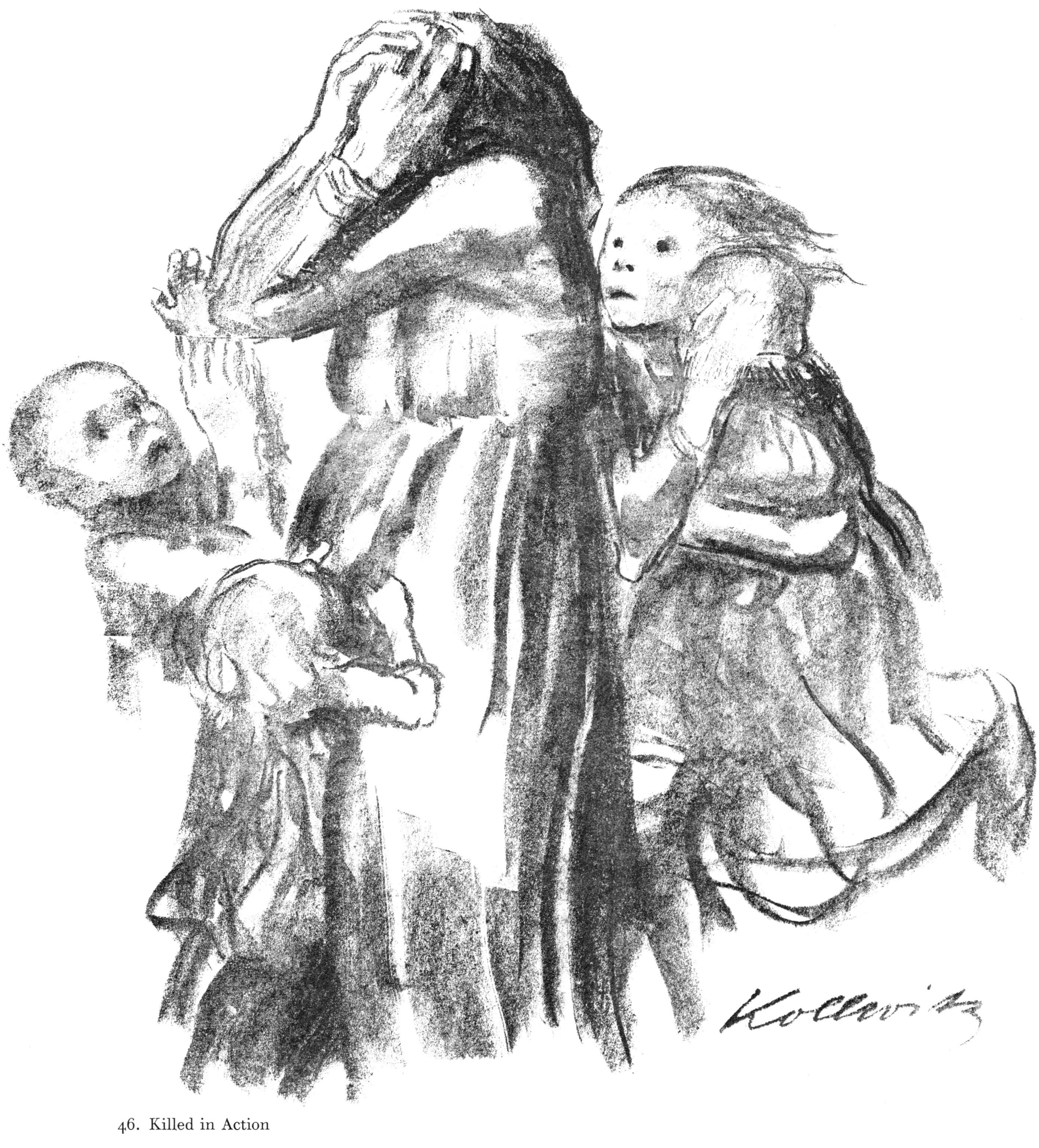

46. Killed in Action

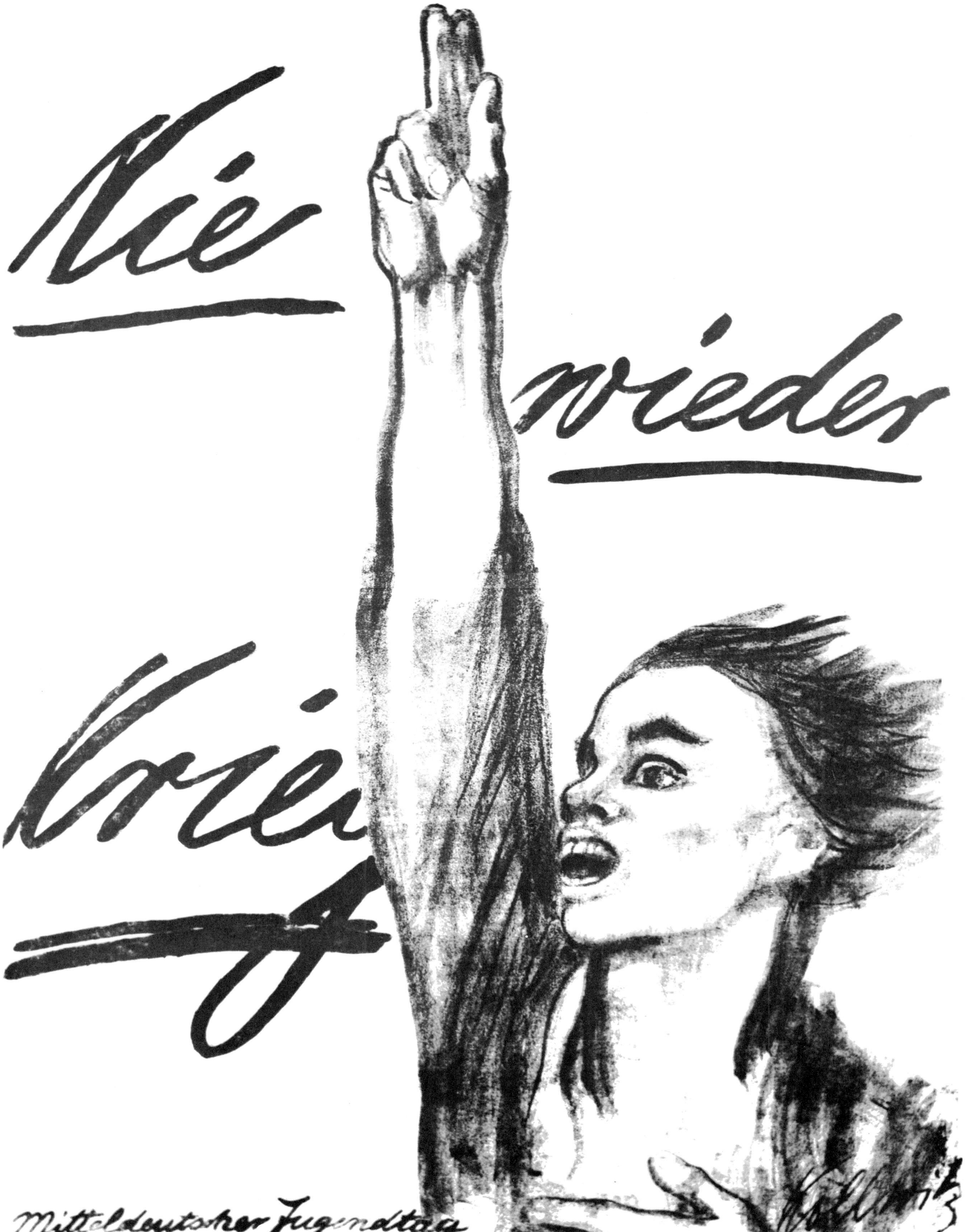

47. Never Again War!

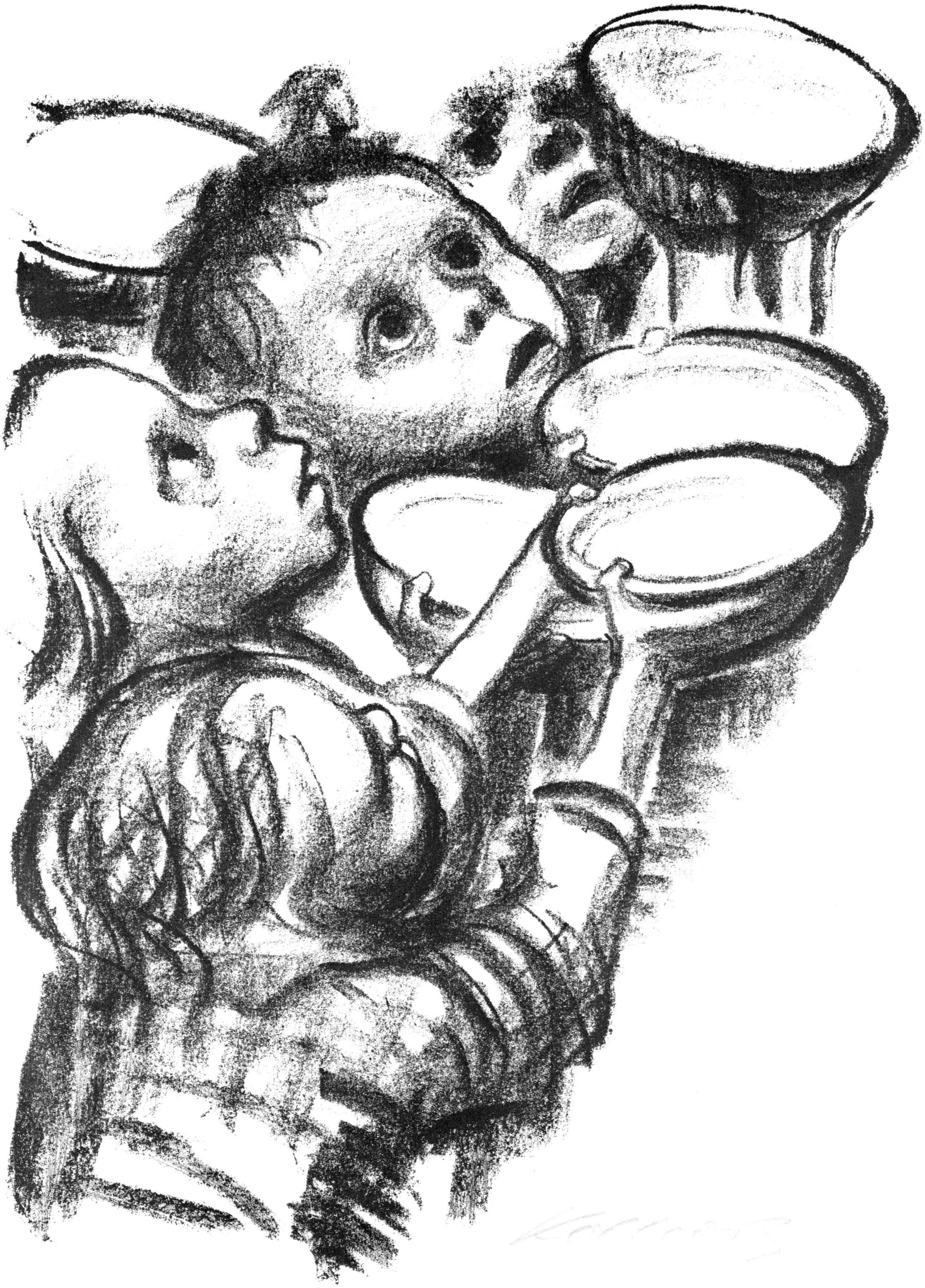

48. Germany's Children Are Starving!

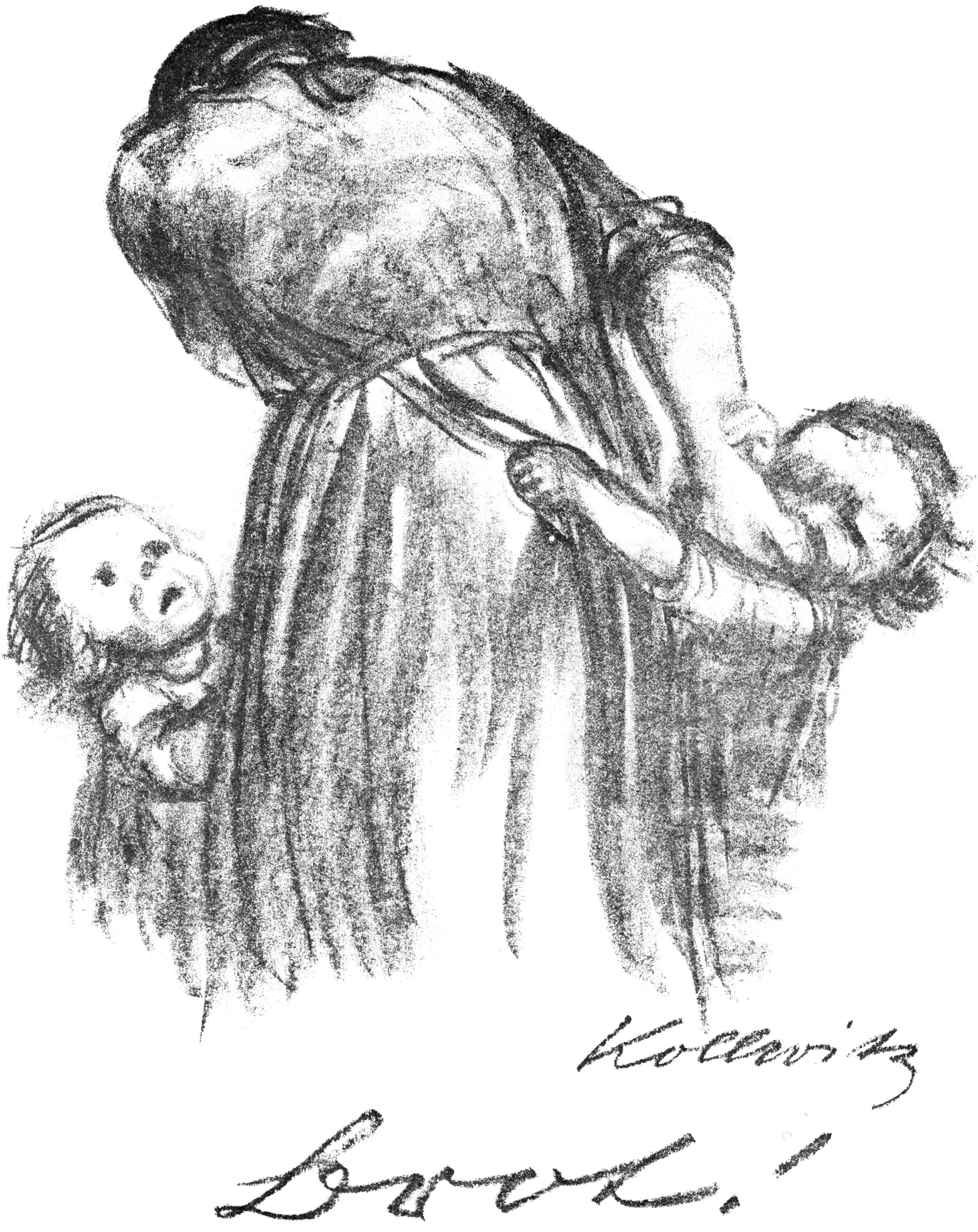

49. Bread!

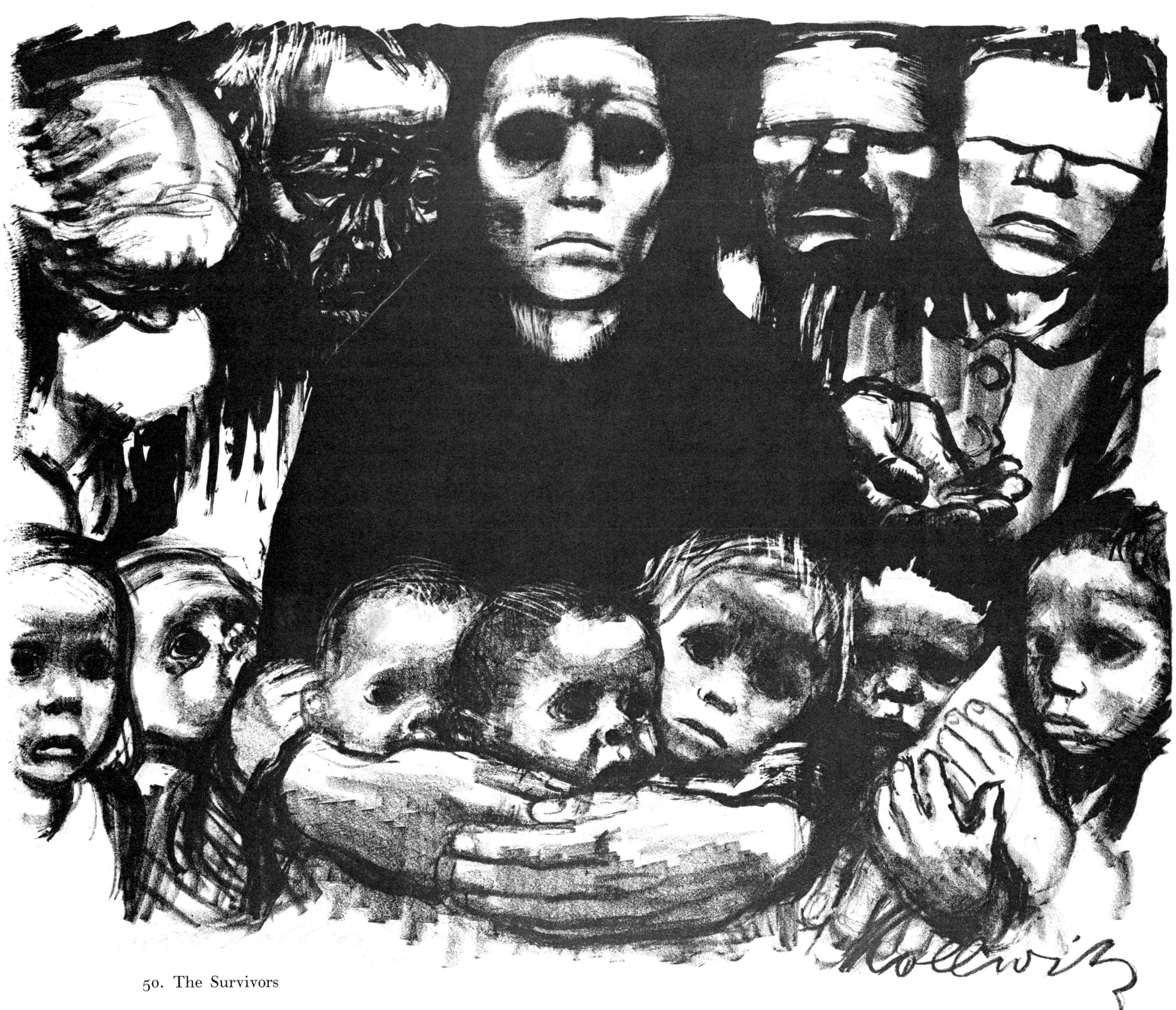

50. The Survivors

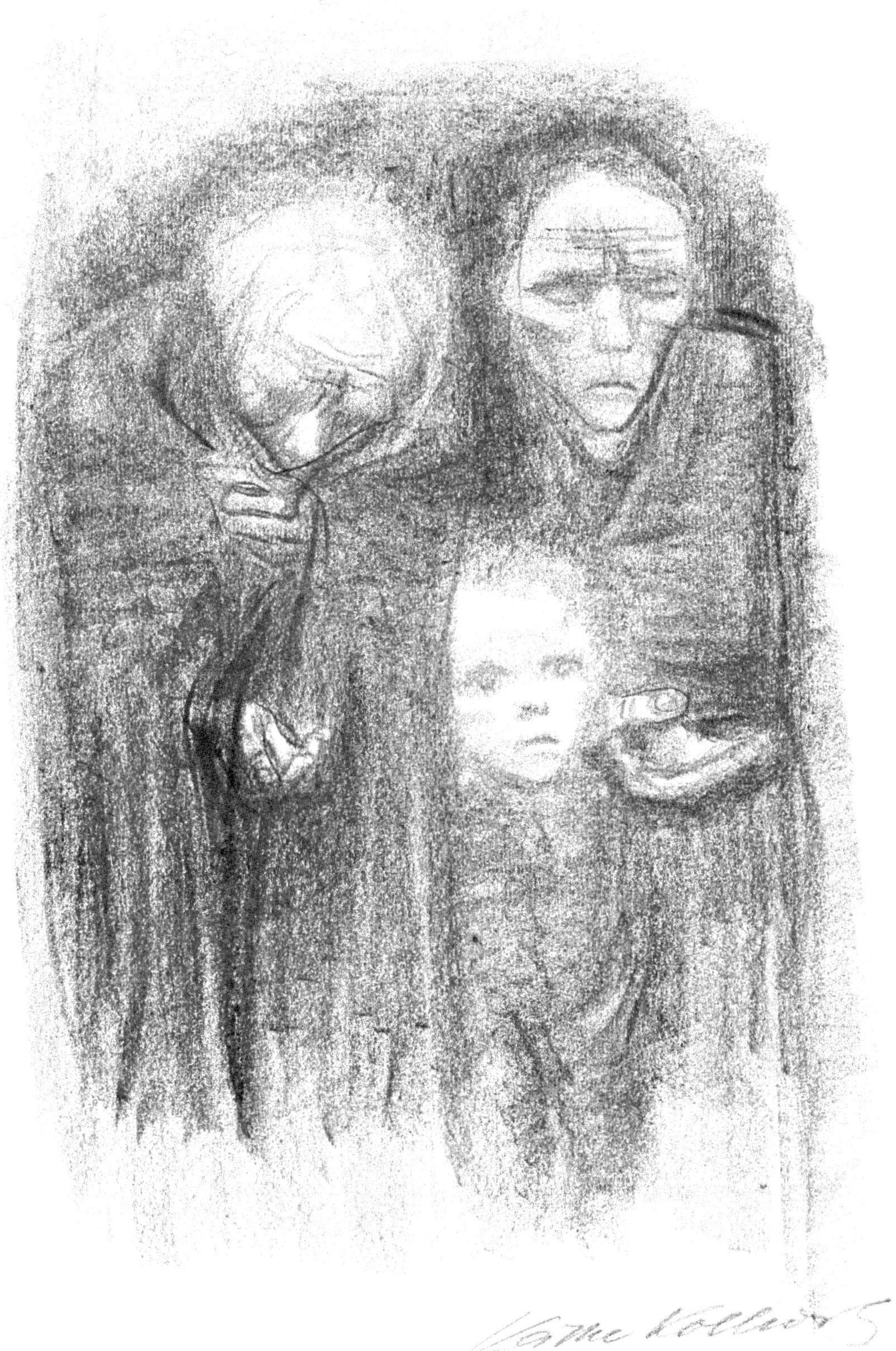

51. Beggars

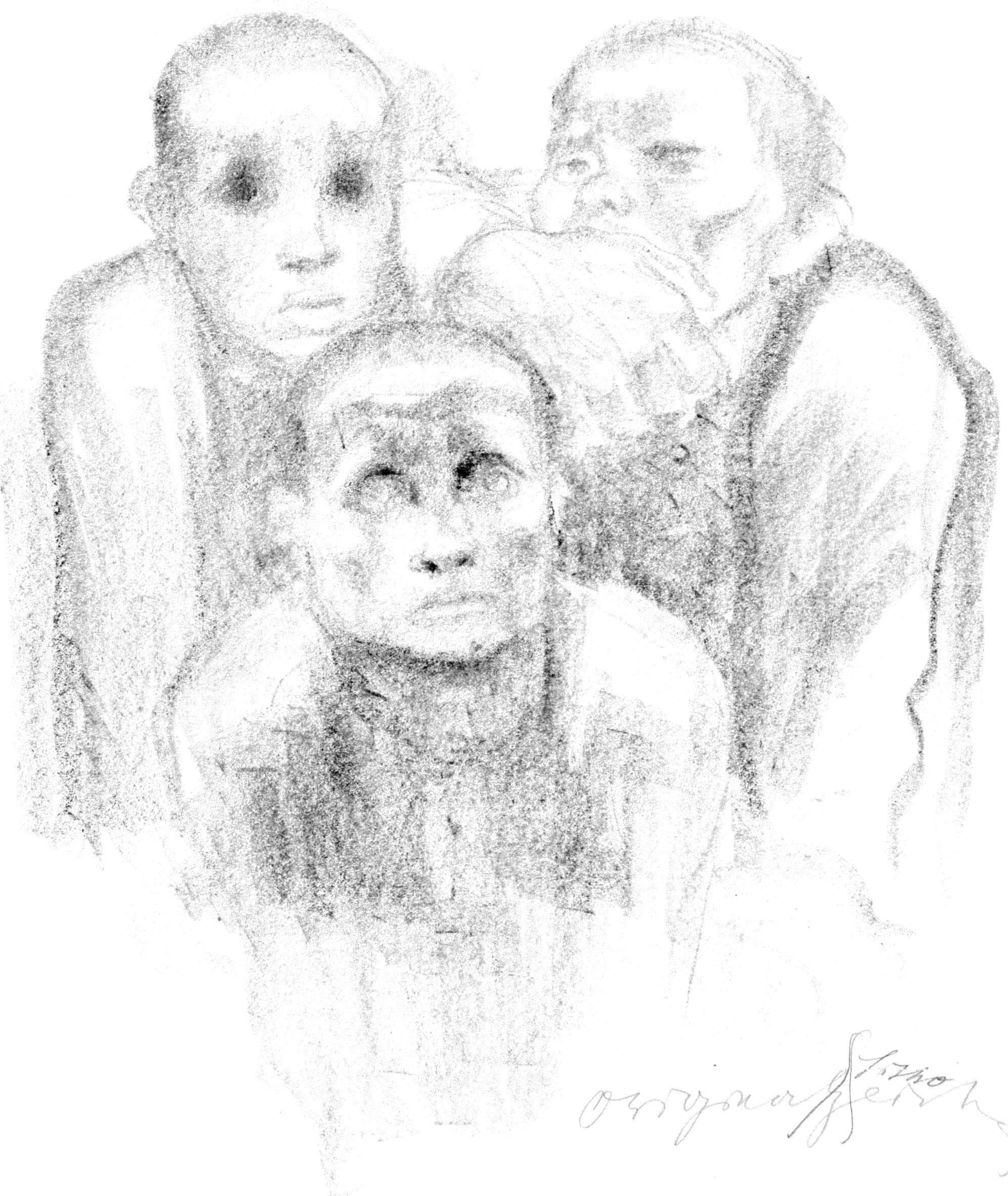

52. Prisoners Listening to Music

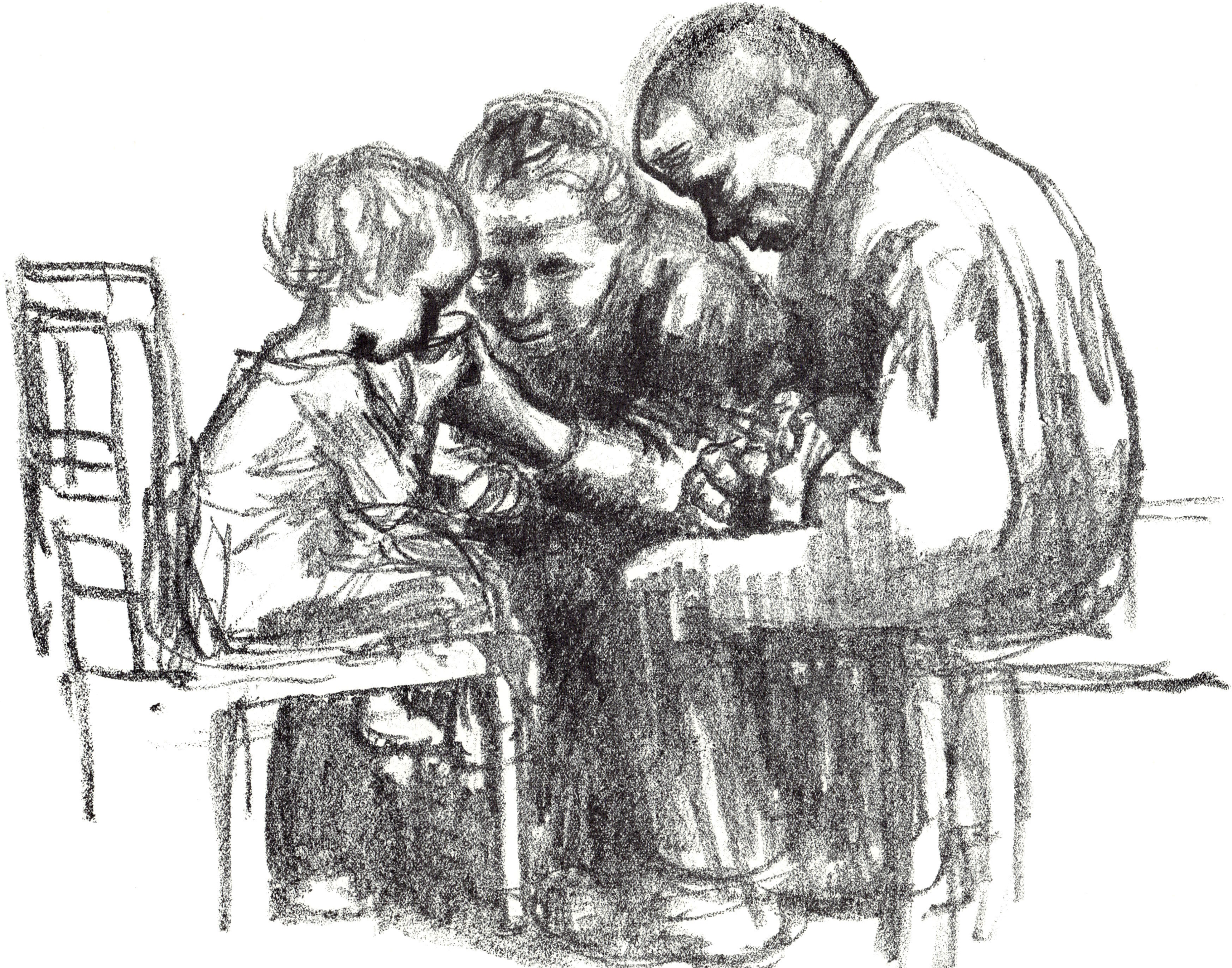

53. Visit to the Children's Hospital

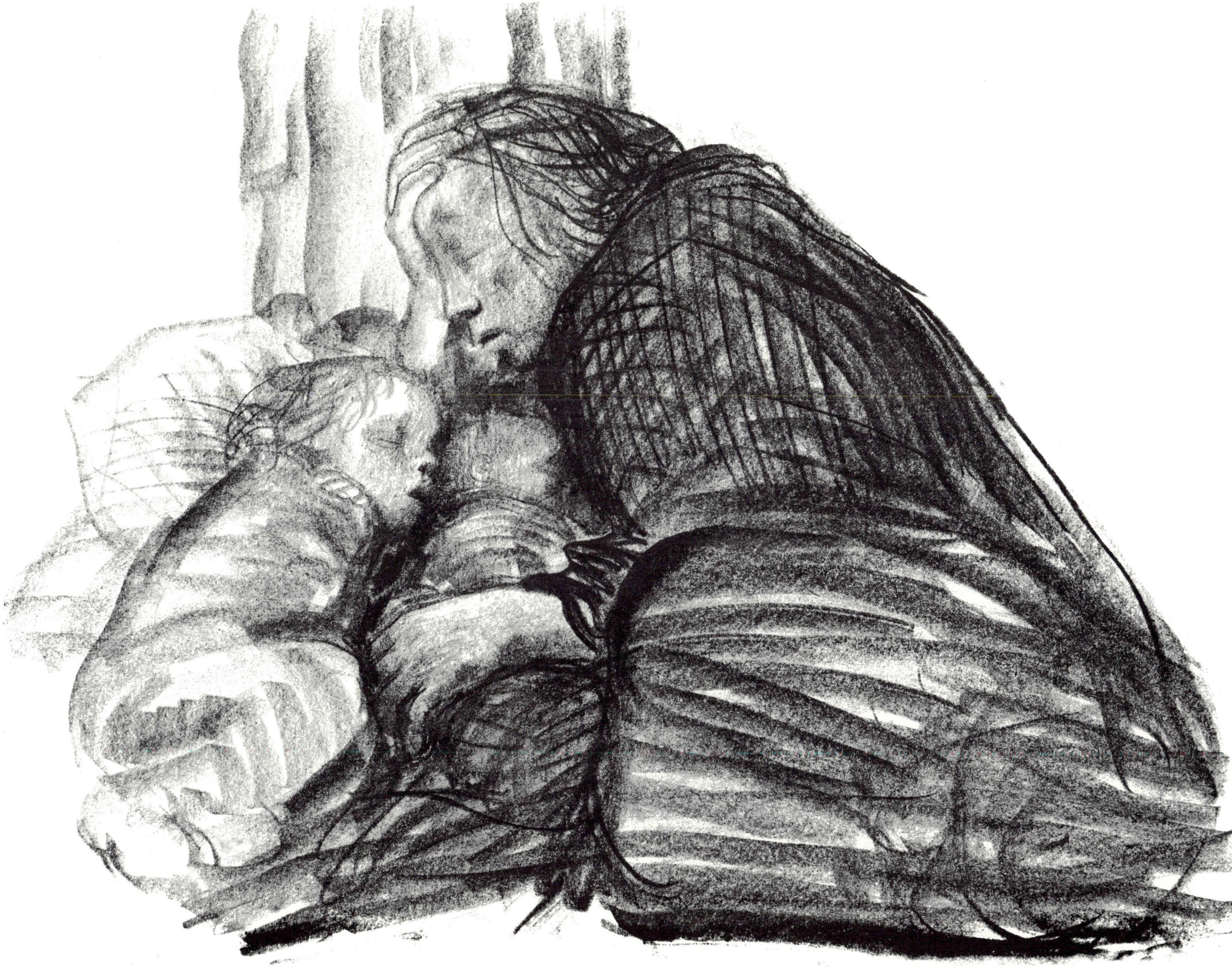

54. Municipal Lodging

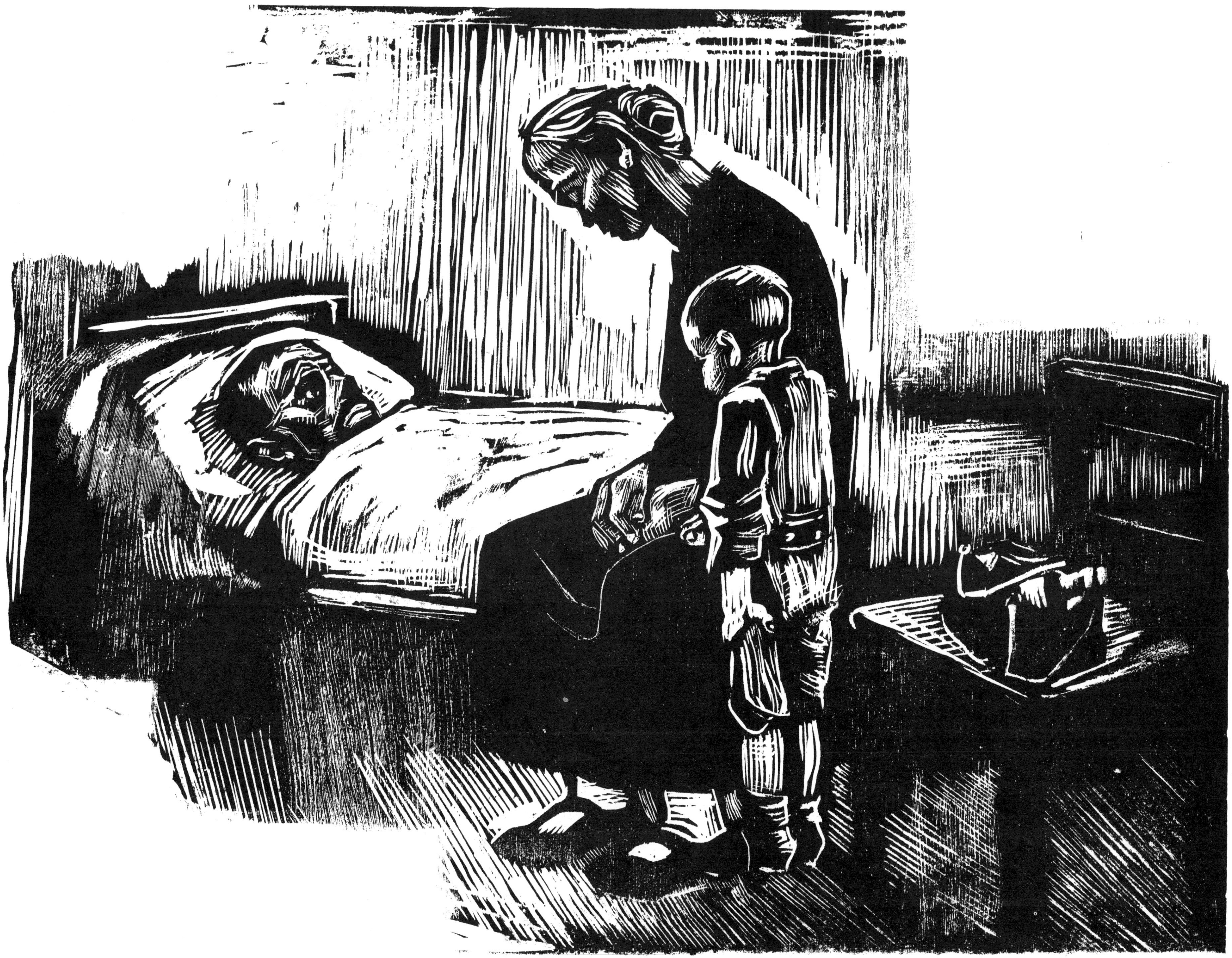

55. Visit to the Hospital

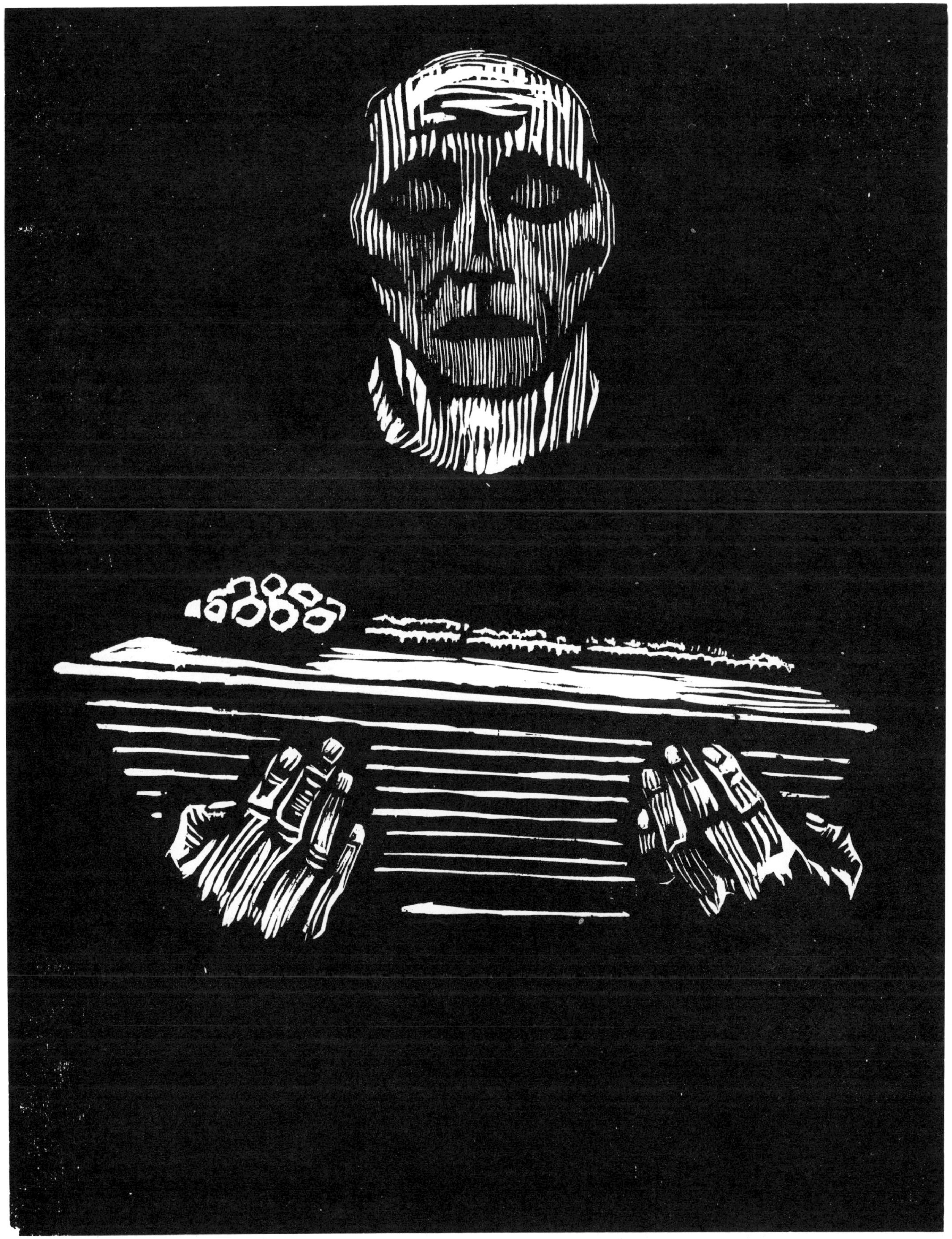

56. Infant Mortality

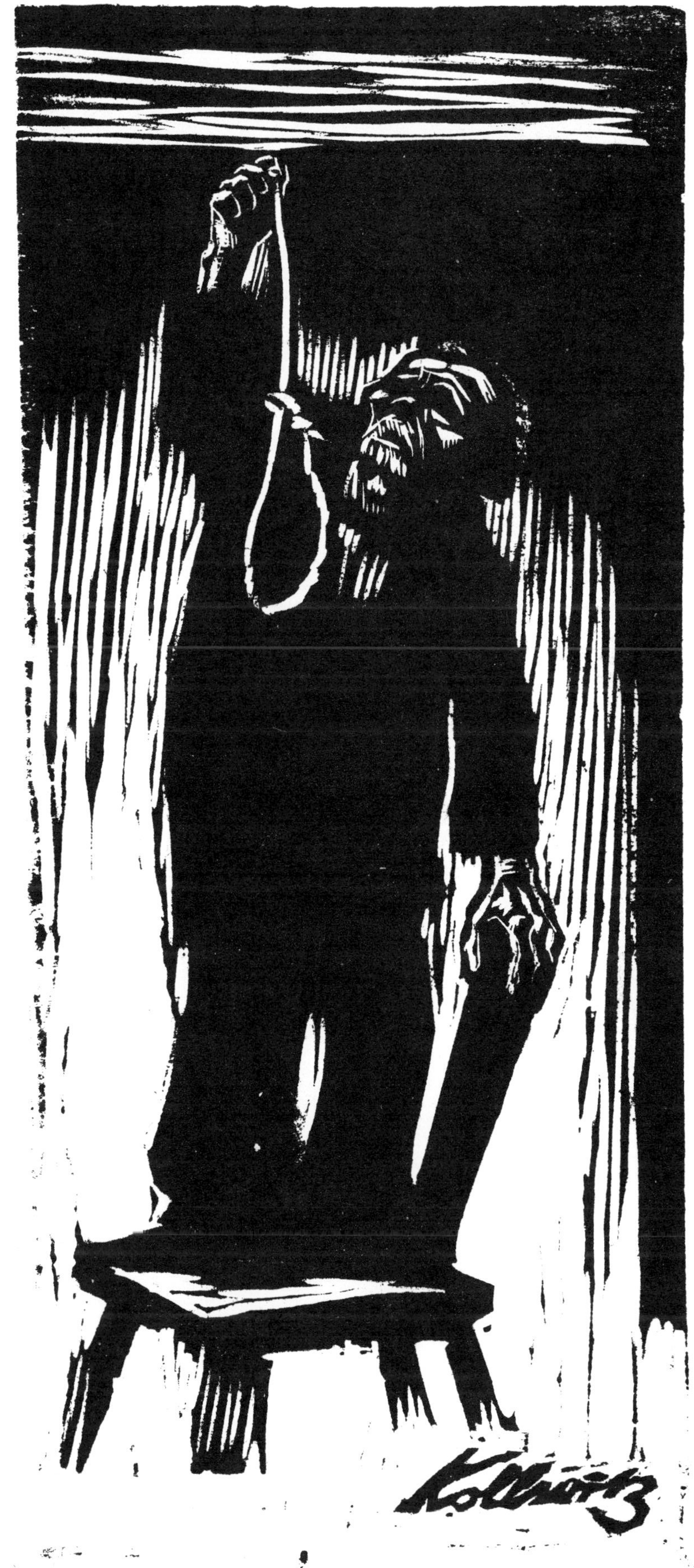

57. The Last Resort

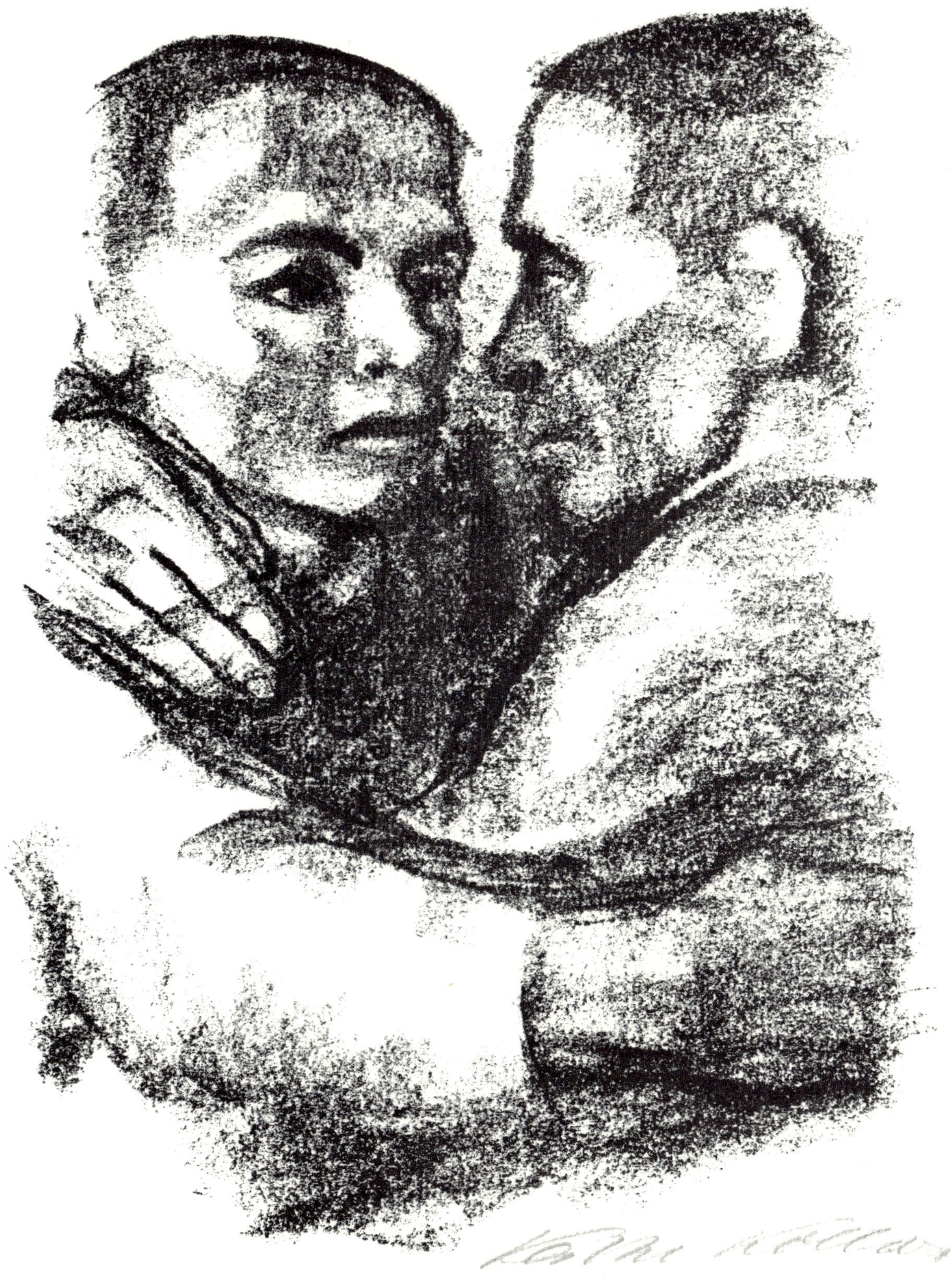

58. Fraternity

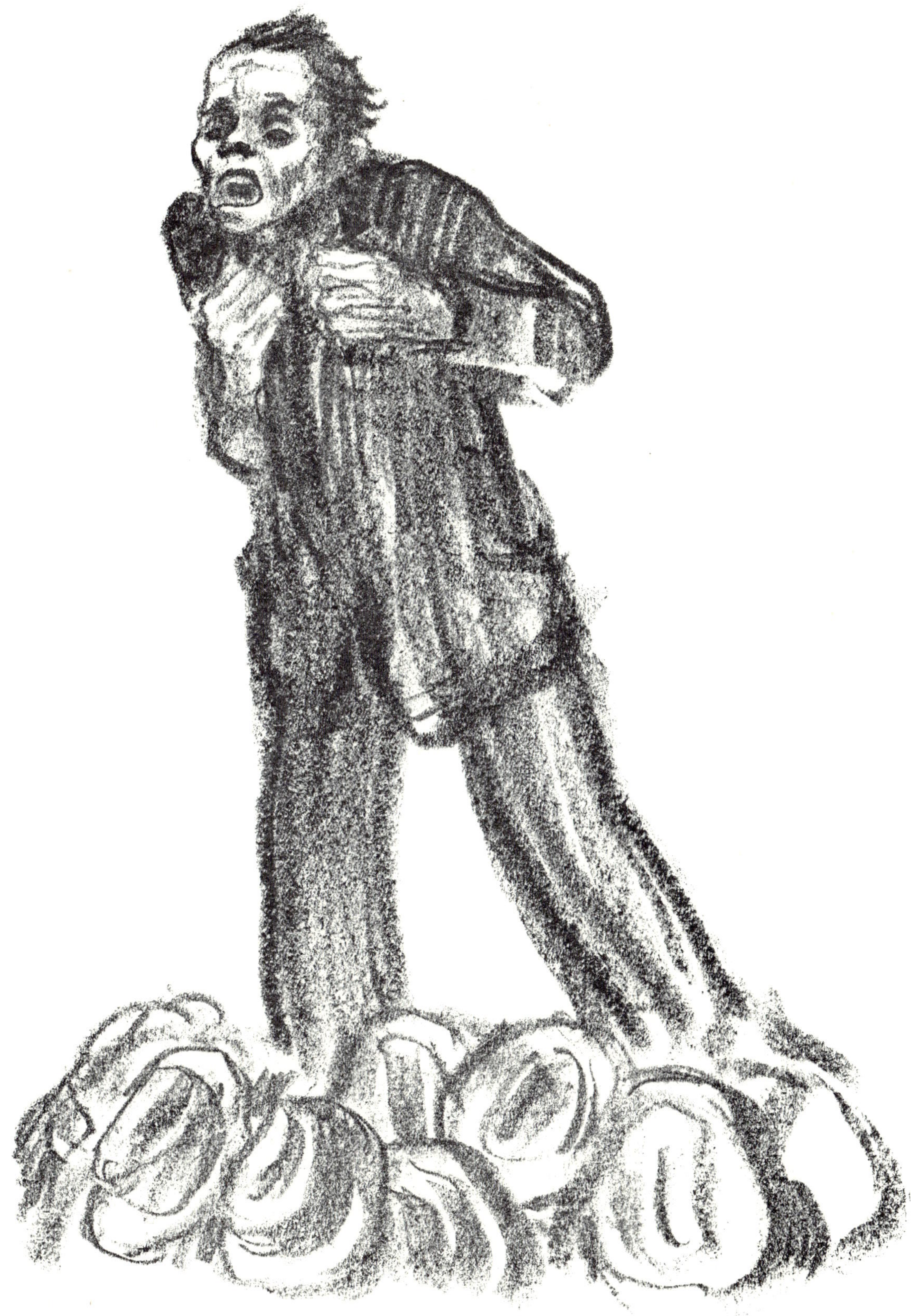

59. The Agitator

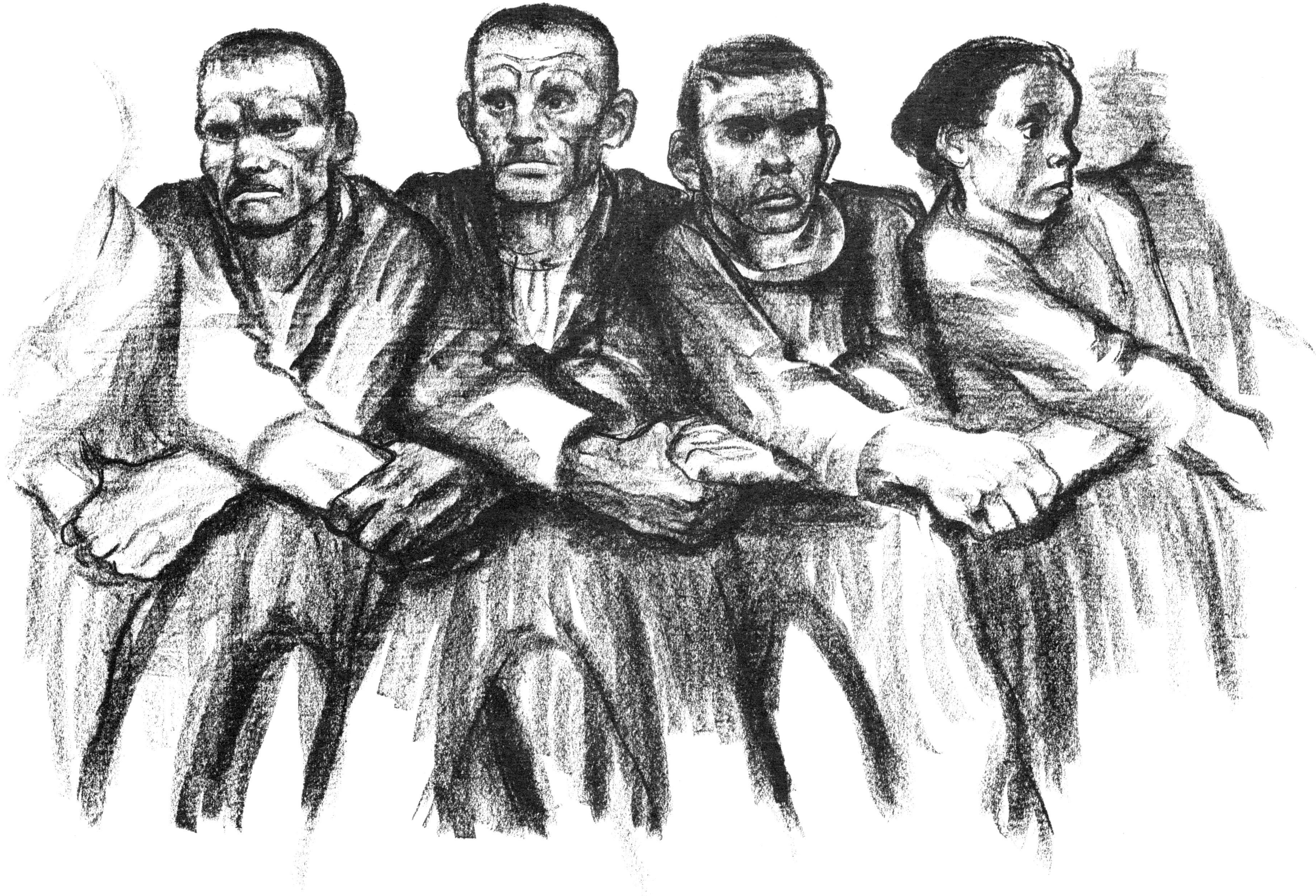

60. Solidarity: The Propeller Song

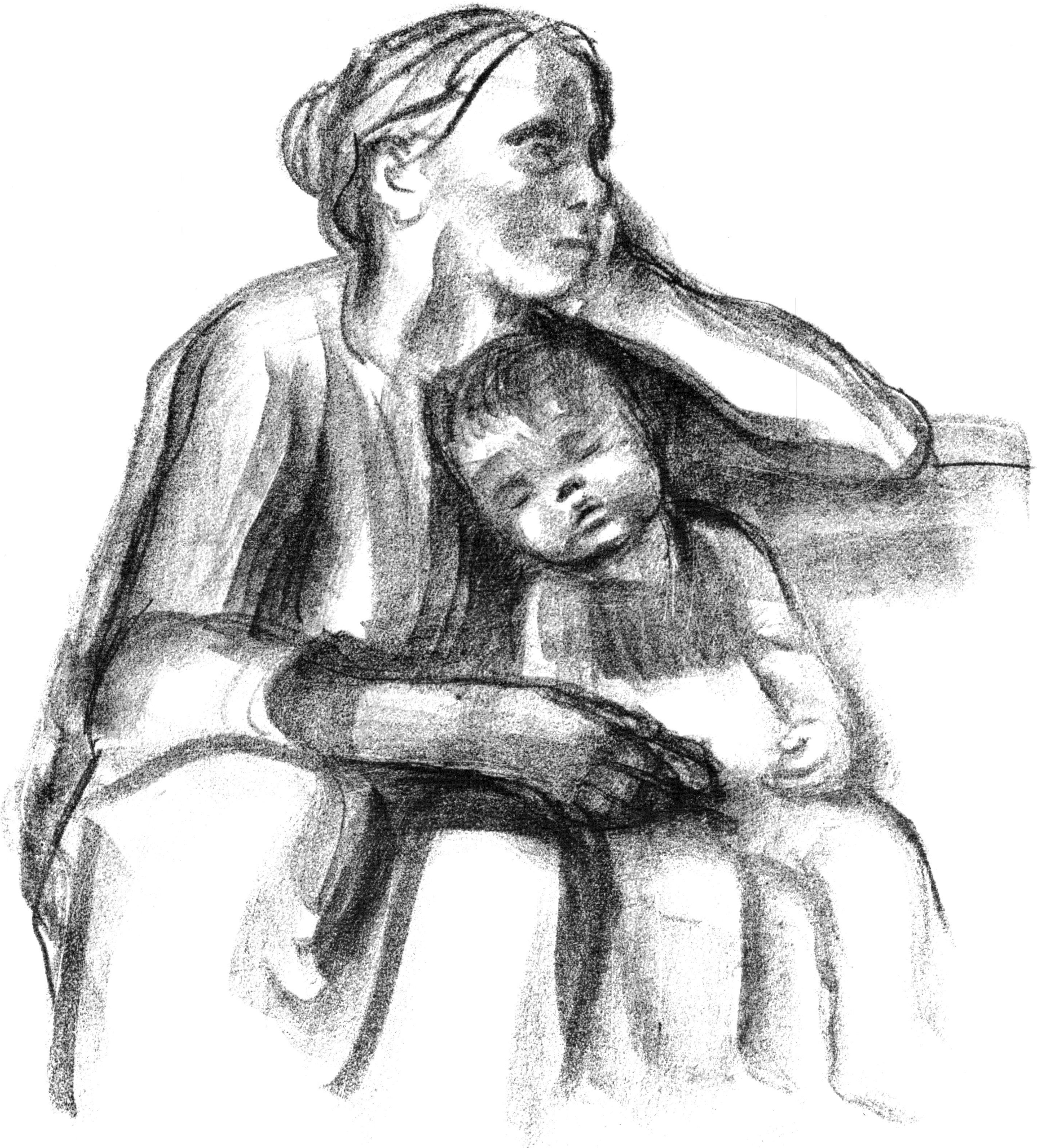

61. Woman with Sleeping Child

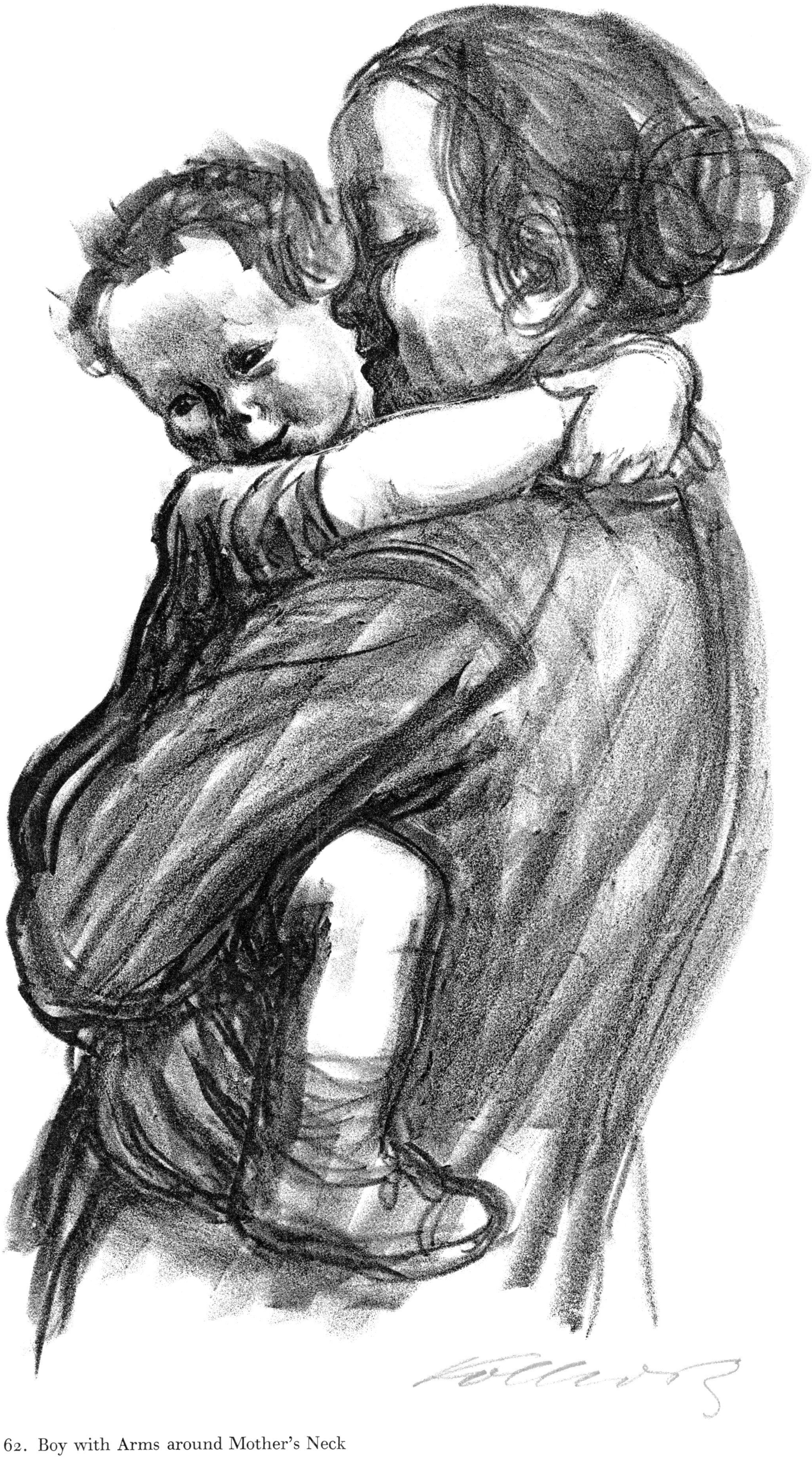

62. Boy with Arms around Mother's Neck

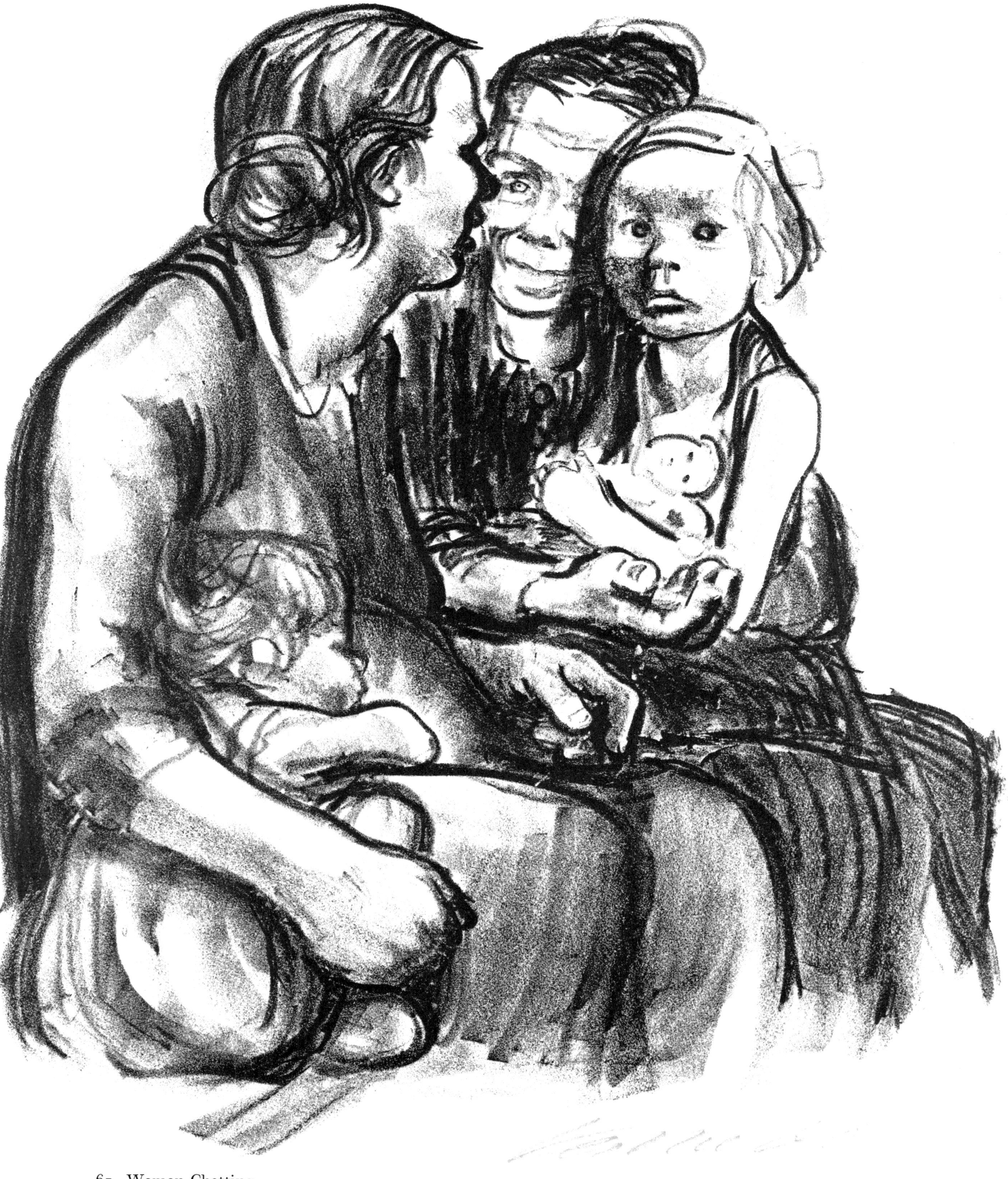

63. Women Chatting

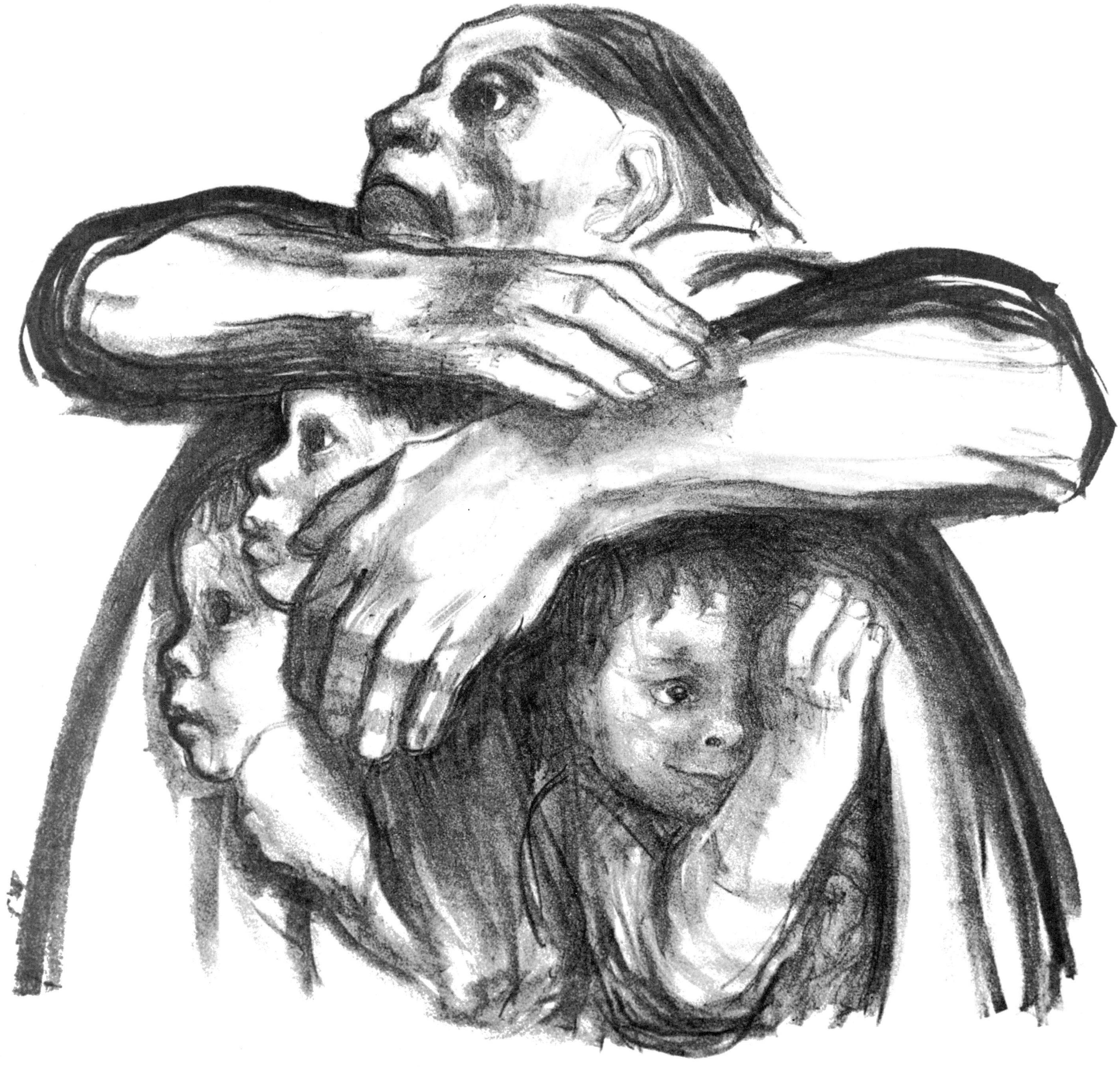

64. Seed Corn Must Not Be Ground

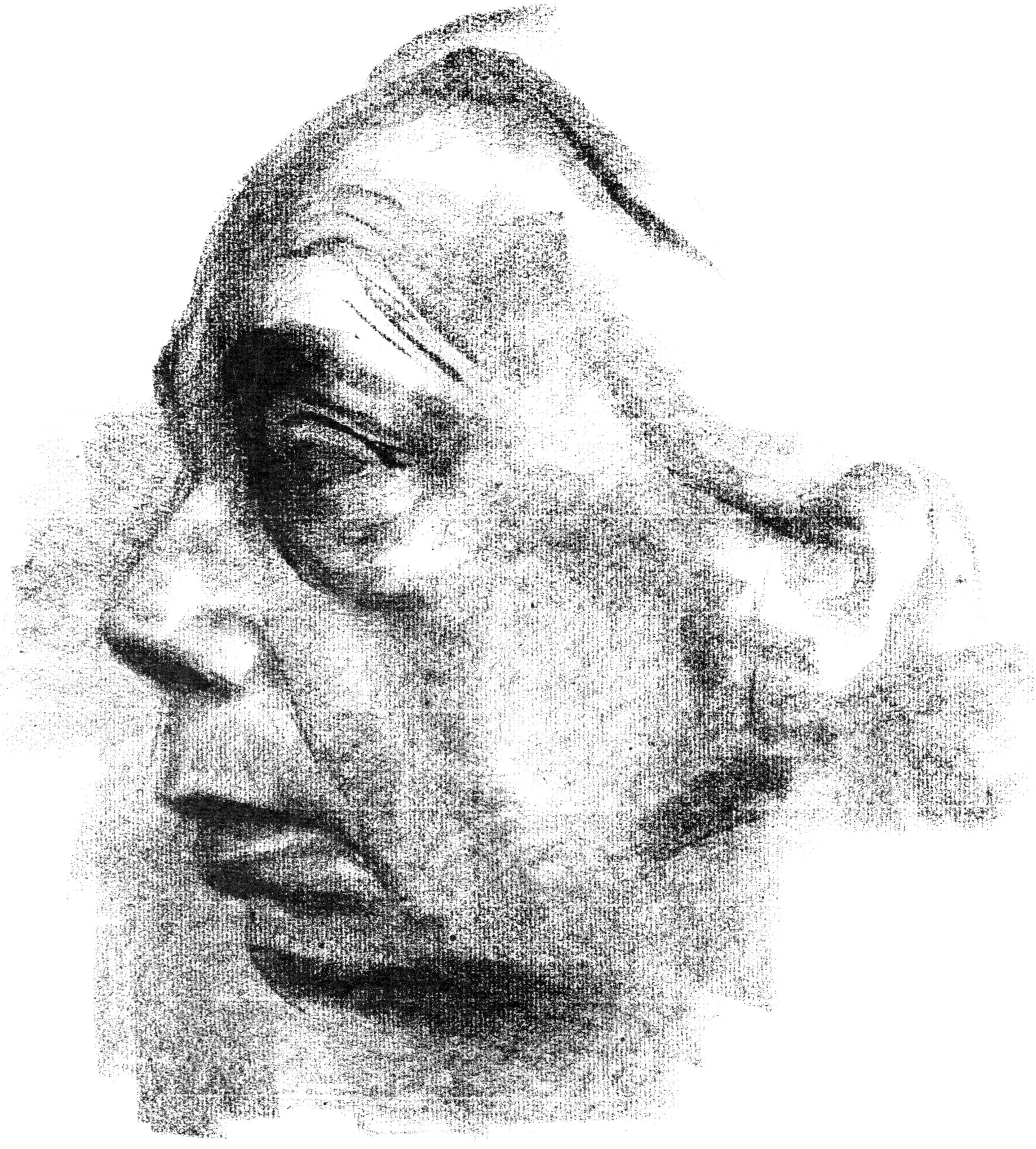

65. Self Portrait, 1927

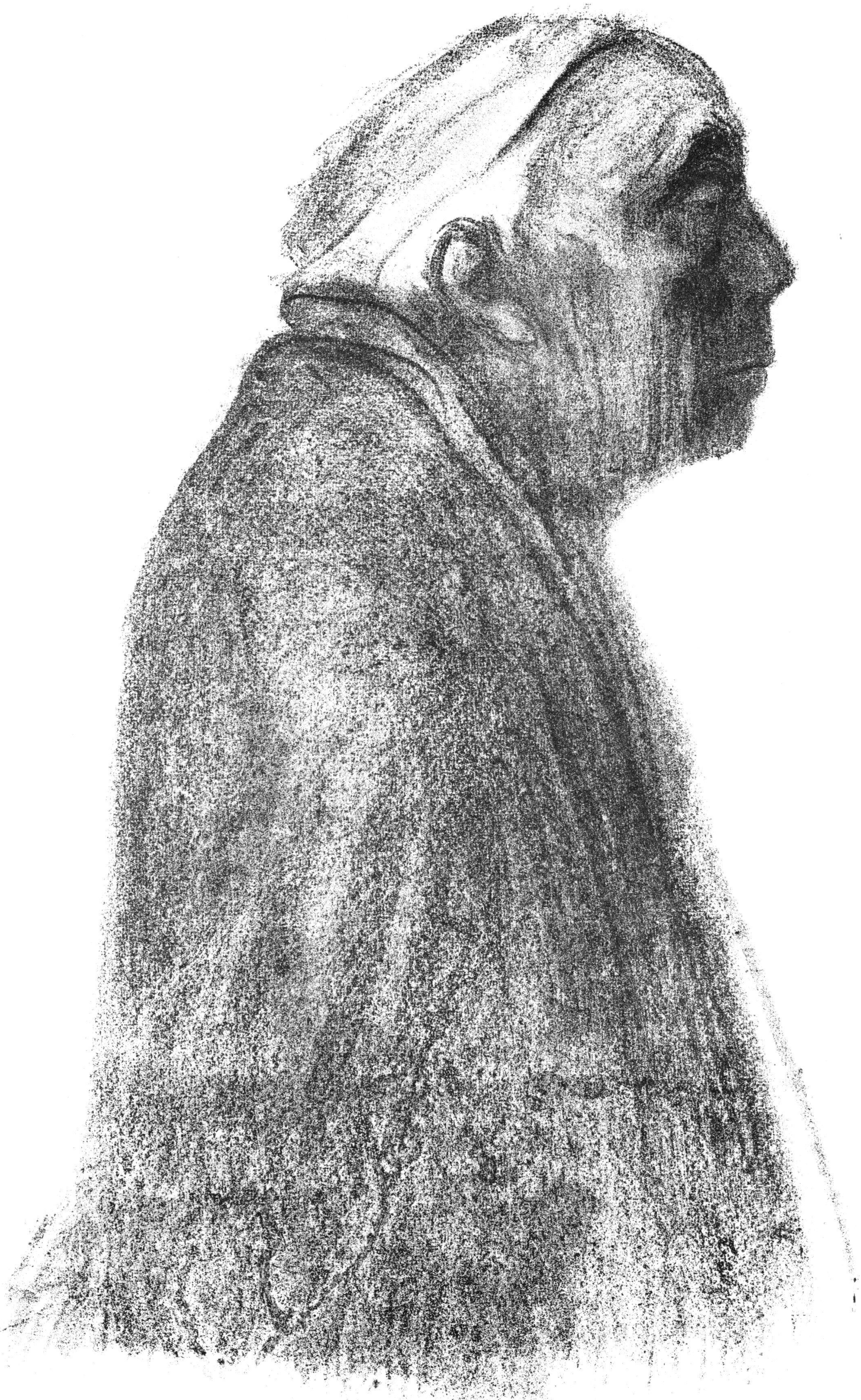

66. Self Portrait, 1938

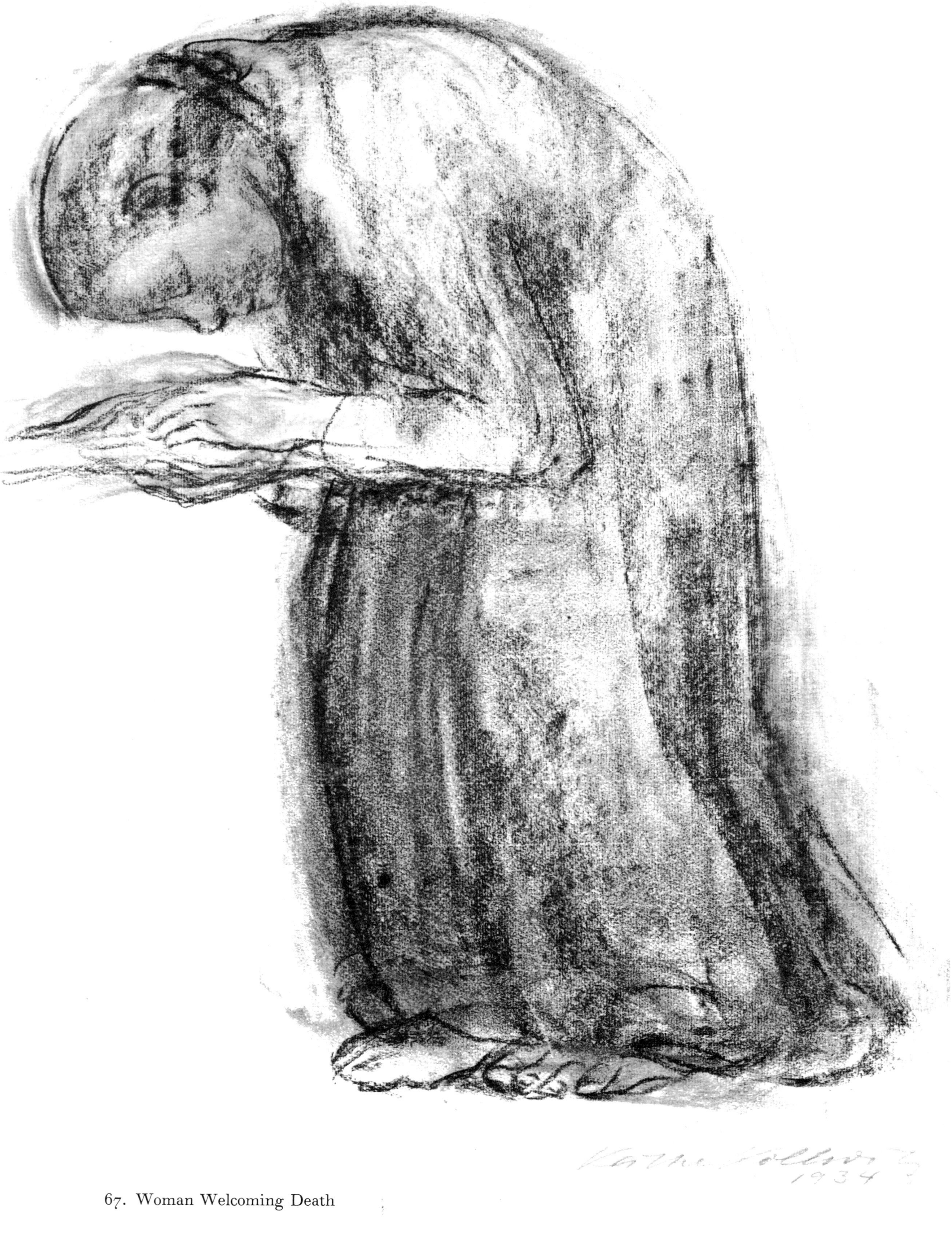

67. Woman Welcoming Death

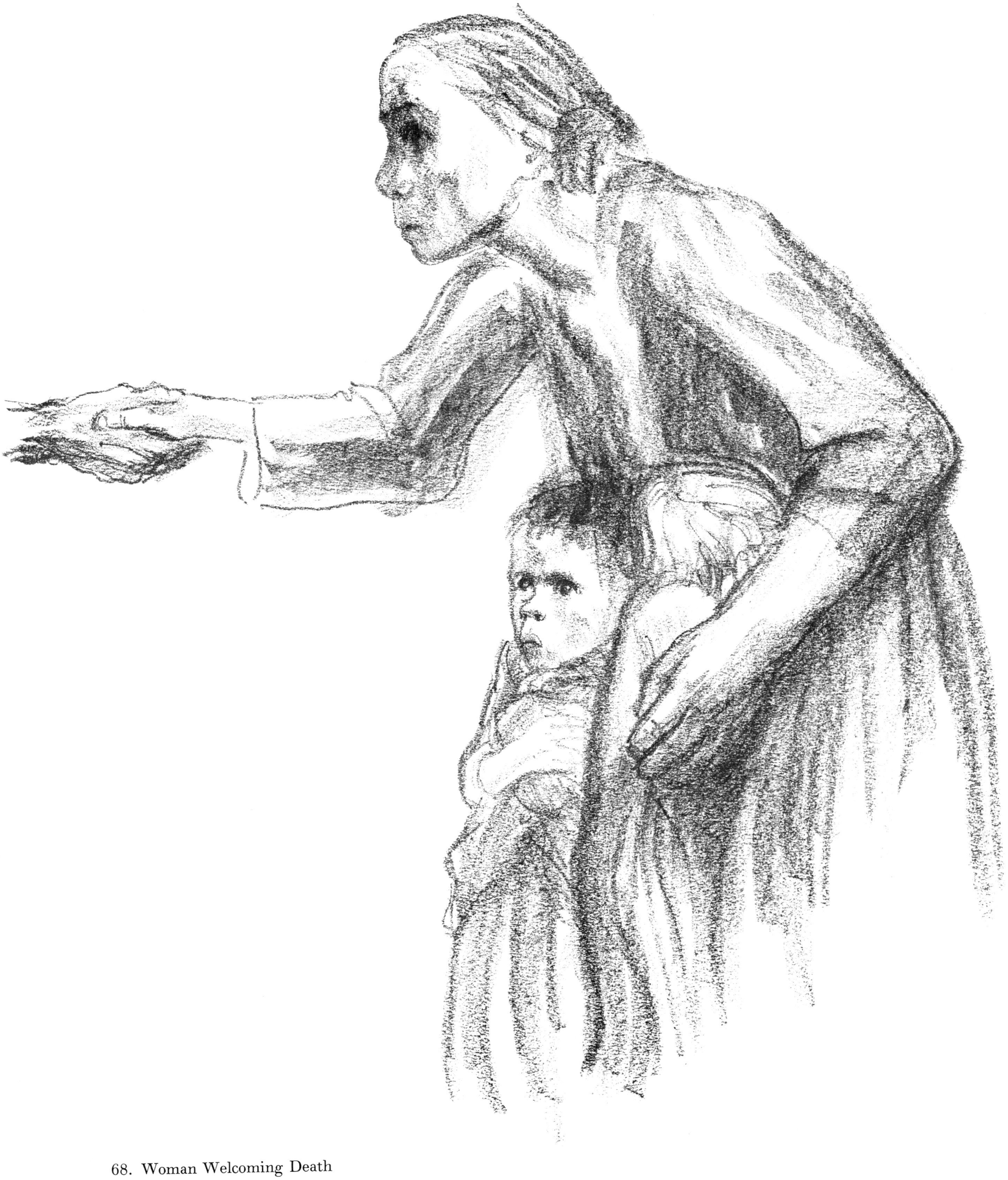

68. Woman Welcoming Death

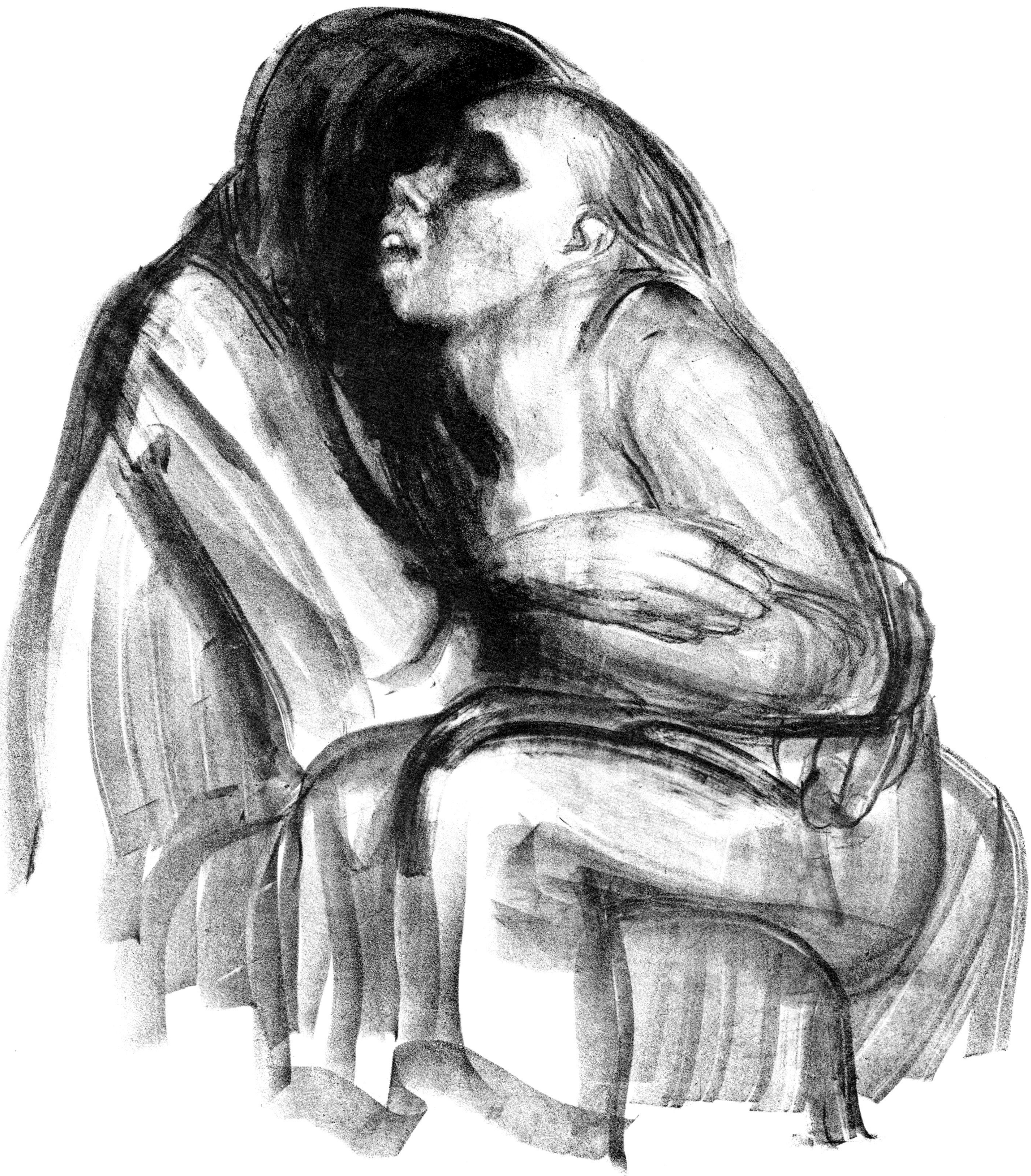

69. Death with Girl in Lap

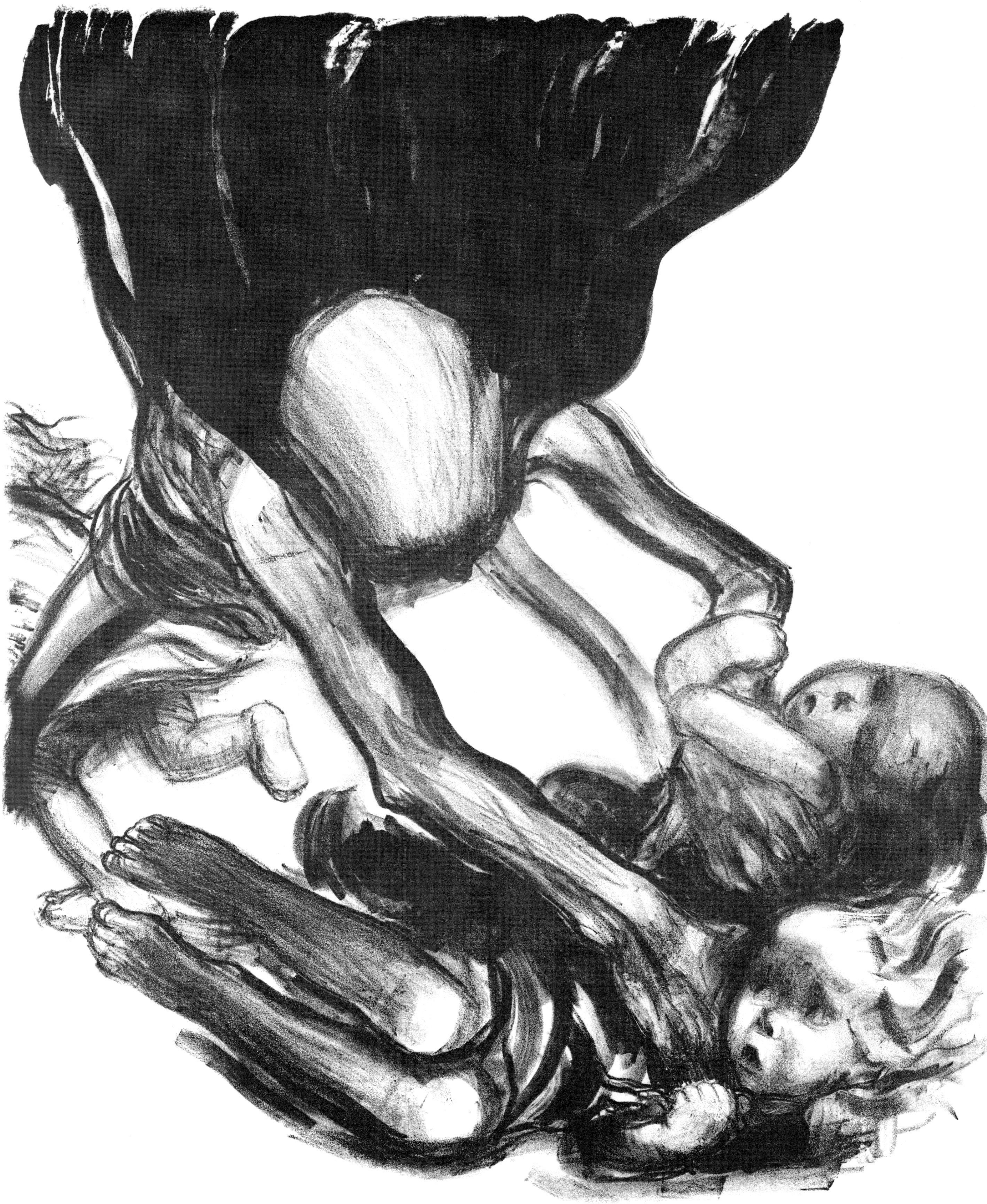

70. Death Swoops

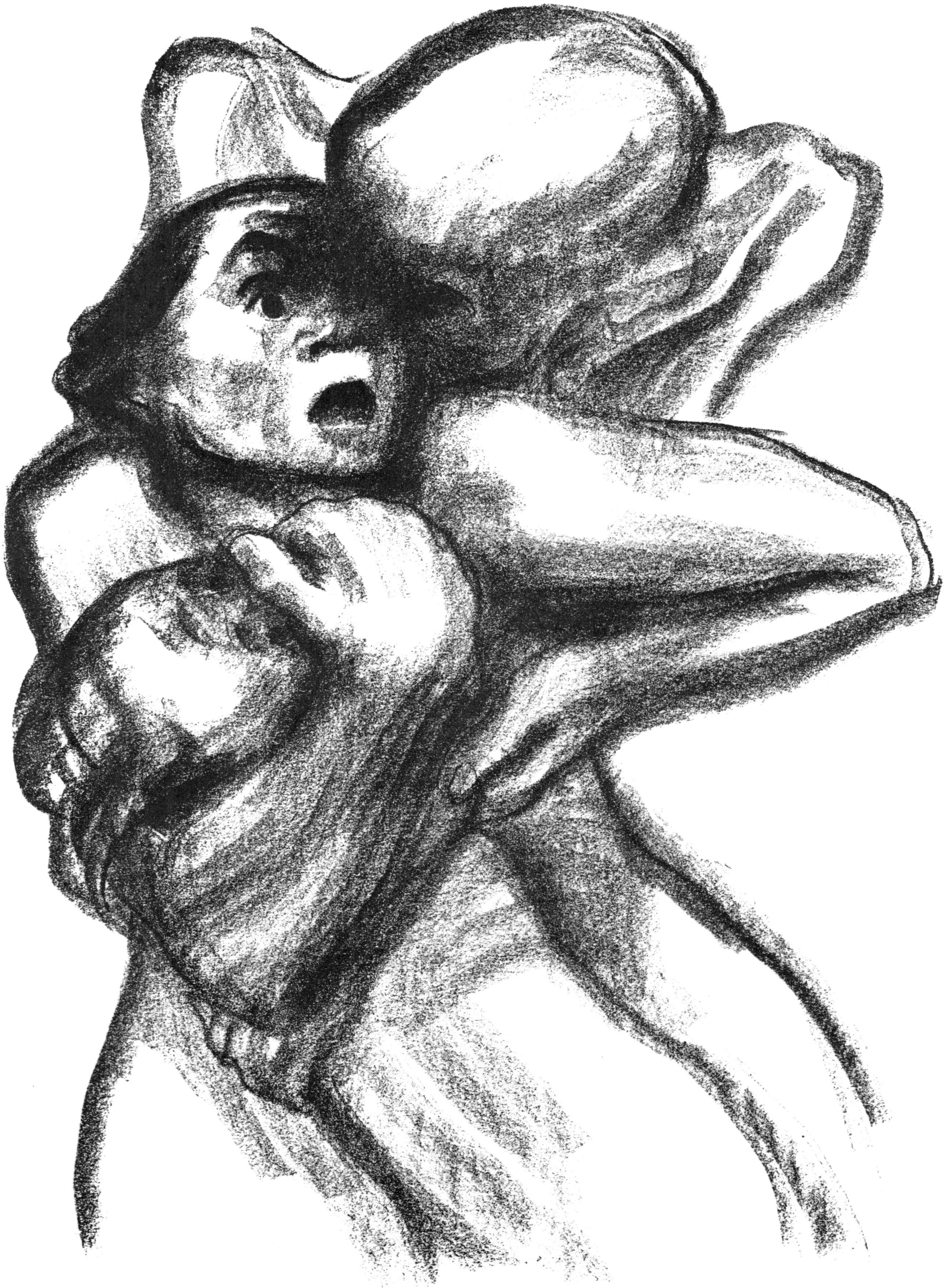

71. Death Seizes a Woman

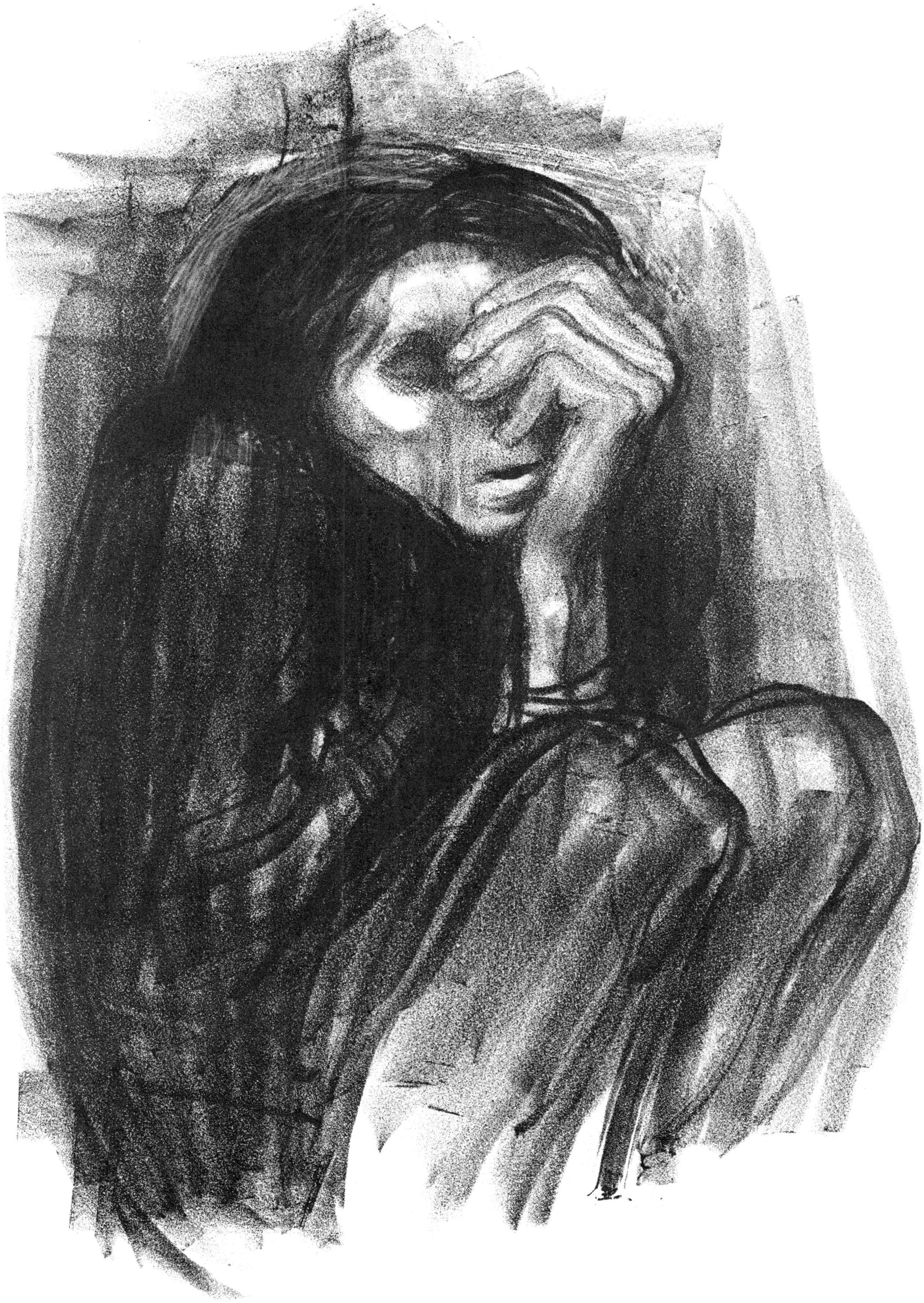

72. Death upon the Highway

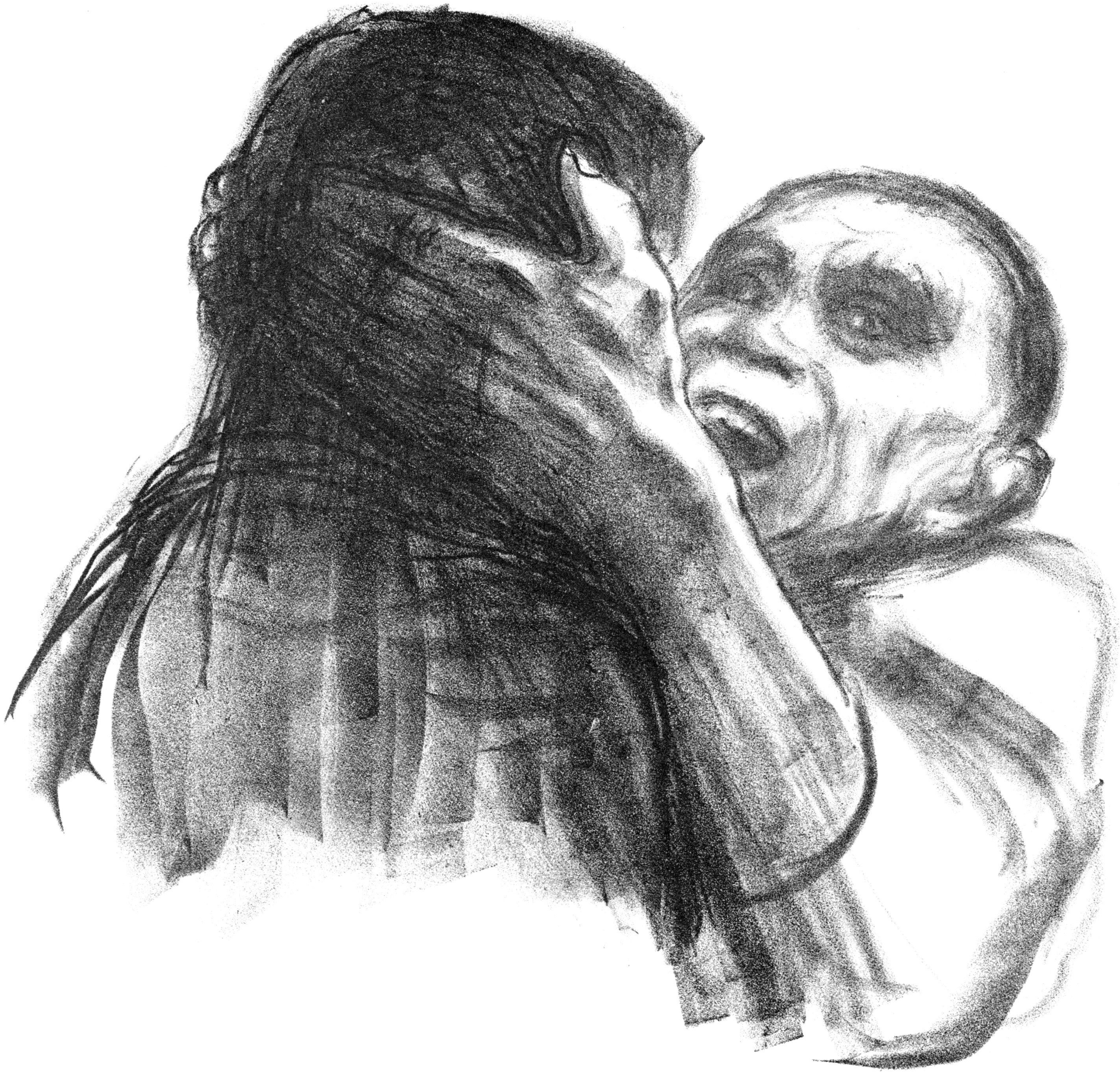

73. Death as a Friend

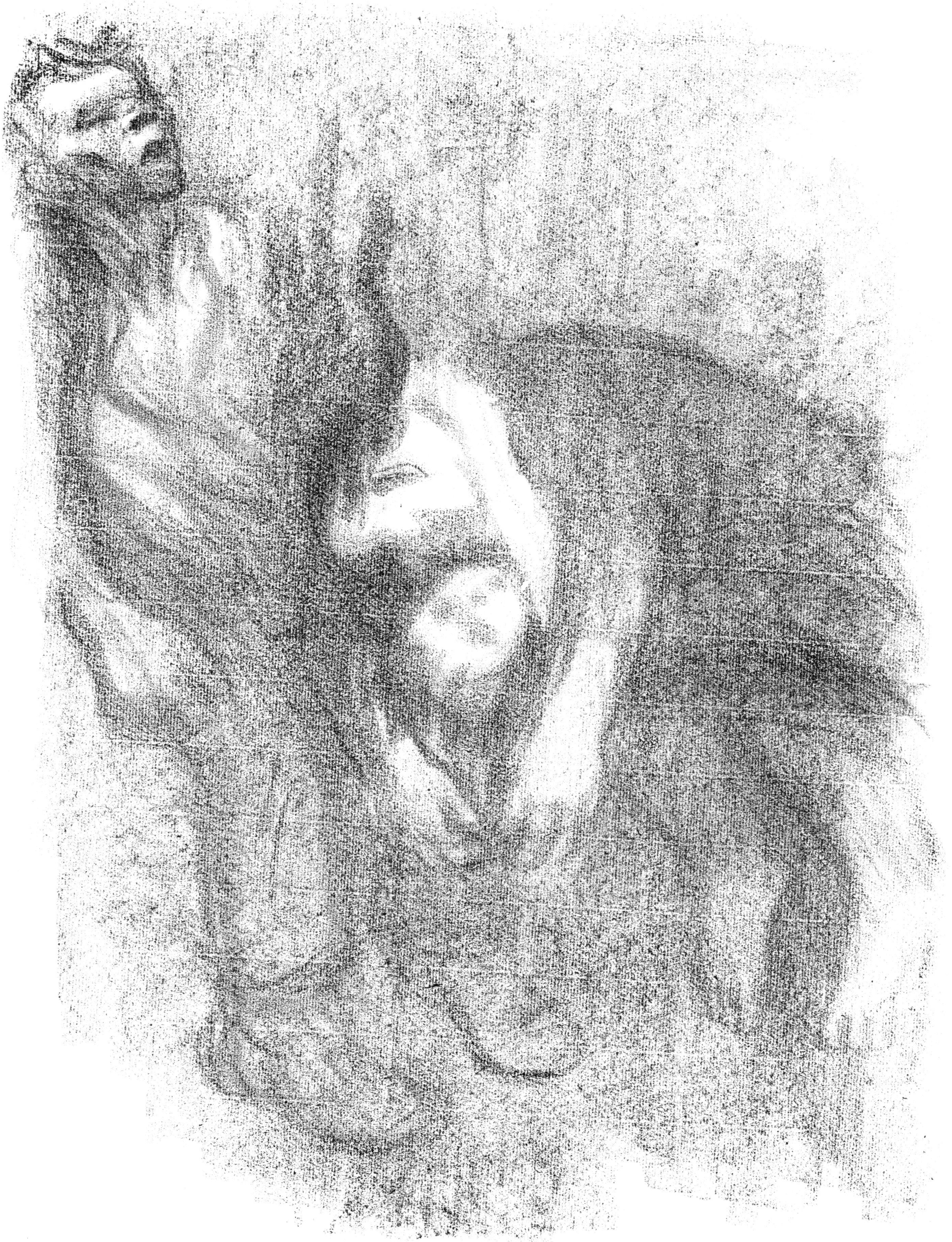

74. Death in the Water

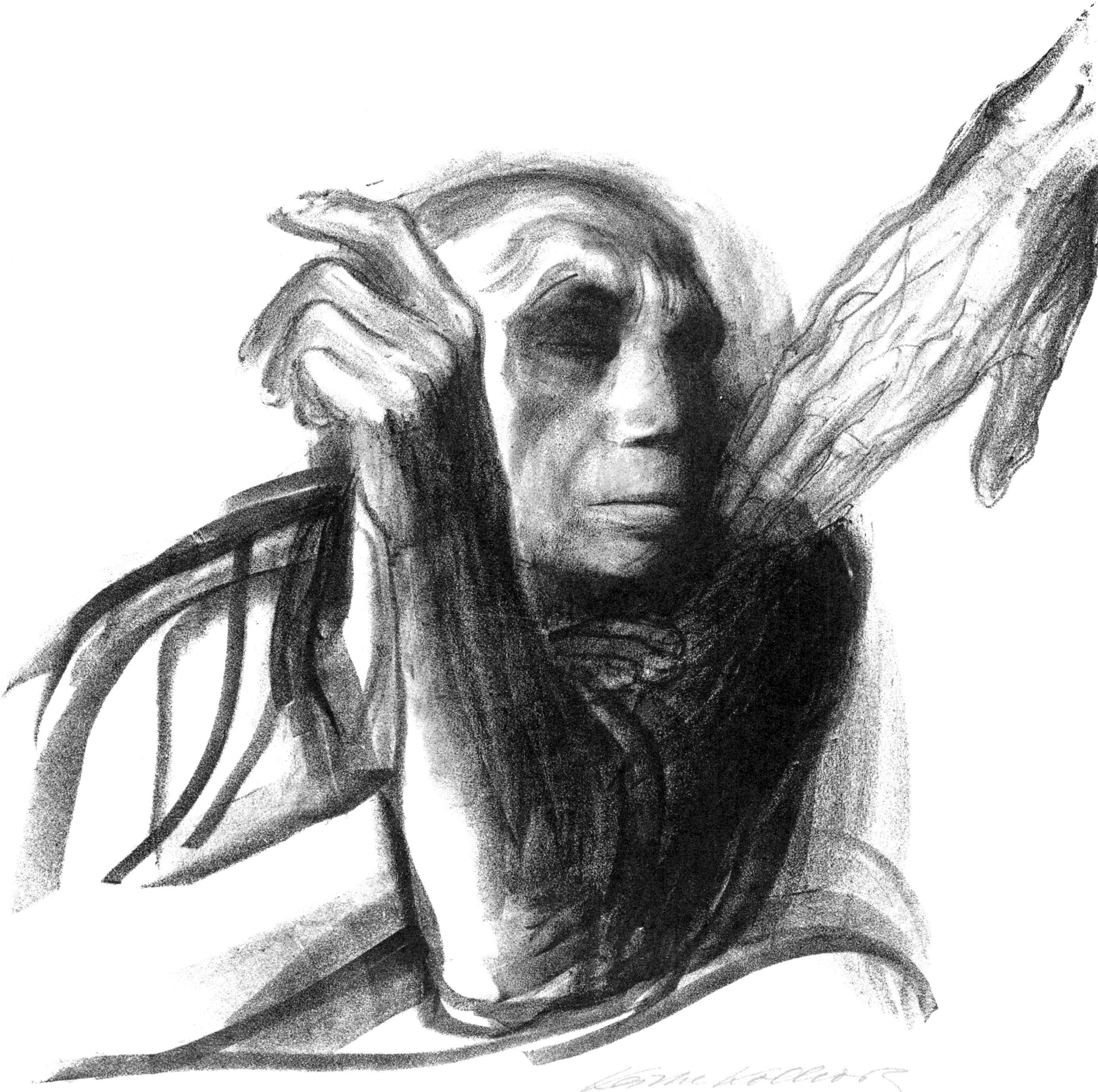

75. The Call of Death